Library of Congress Catalog Numder: 92-072895

ISBN: 0-9633609-0-6

For additional copies of this book contact:

INNSIDE PRESS
P.O. Box 584
Bayfield, WI 54814

Printed in USA by
Palmer Publications, Inc.
Amherst, WI 54406

Dedication

This book is dedicated to our mothers, or as we refer to them, "mom", and "moms".

June Colton Mitchell Stuessy

Margaret Ann Phillips

Together, they represent a rich mixture of heartland backgrounds with an equally varied collection of foods.

They were raised in a time of self-sufficiency. Their ingredients were most often gathered or grown, the humble gifts and bounty from around them.

To these they added their particular senses of taste and together created a treasury of good foods.

Their inspirations are forever a part of us.

June Colton Michell Stuessy

Mary May

Margaret Ann Phillips

Joan

John

Joe

Jim

Jerry

Janice

Jean

Jill

Julie

Jeff

Acknowledgments

Katherine Purcell introduced us, as university students, to French cooking. Her meals are with us today, as well as the wonderful times we shared with her and her husband, Mark.

Ed Freeman played "devil's advocate" for seemingly endless hours as we debated the move to Bayfield and the transition into innkeeping. Finally, exhausted, we said, "maybe you're right, it probably wasn't such a great idea"; whereupon he said, "no, it is a great idea, it's a fabulous idea . . . and I want to be your first guest."

Lois Albrecht, as co-worker and co-dreamer, planted the idea of a cookbook and nurtured it for years. Lois, with the two of us, formed the nucleous of our staff for years; and she formulated and/or brought to fruition many ideas. Our gratitude is enormous.

Mary Rice has always encouraged us to dream, to create, to evaluate, and then to dream again.

Bob and Norma Schaub endlessly continue to open our minds to new food experiences on our travels together. They also possess that rare quality of being able to offer both encouragement and creative criticism with honesty and love.

Susan Larsen, friend and co-worker, exemplifies our ideal of the Innkeeper. She is a continuous source of inspiration which is richly supported by talent and energy. But it is her warmth of heart, her deep love of people which is so much a part of her life and who she is that makes her truly unique.

Photography and Illustration Credits

Photography

Illustrations

Old Rittenhouse Inn
Published Recipes

"Recipes From Great American Inns", *Benson & Hedges,* n.d.
>Strawberry Consommé

Mimi Elder, "Inns of the Midwest", *Gourmet,* March 1985
>Cheese Pie (Wisconsin Cheese Pie)
>Lemon Cheesecake with Glazed Raspberries
>Onion Dill Bread
>Raspberry Soup
>Red Raspberry Cordial

"Christmas at a Country Inn", *Better Homes and Gardens,* Holiday Cooking, 1986
>Maple Walnut Pie
>Red Raspberry Cordial
>Red Raspberry Truffle
>Stuffed Mushrooms

Tom Davis, "Creating a Stir", *Wisconsin Trails,* November/December 1987
>Onion Dill Bread

Anne Crooks, "Old Rittenhouse Inn", *Midwest Living,* June 1987
>Orange Blossom Torte

"Specialties from Country Inns", *Better Homes and Gardens,* Holiday Desserts, 1988
>Maple Walnut Pie
>Red Raspberry Truffles

Kitty and Lucian Maynard, *Country Inns and Bed & Breakfast Cookbook,* (Tennessee, Rutledge Hill Press, 1989)
>Onion Dill Bread
>Rittenhouse Cheese Pie (Wisconsin Cheese Pie)
>Strawberry Consommé

Laura Zahn, *Wake Up & Smell the Coffee,* (Minnesota, Down to Earth Publications, 1988)
>Apple Cider Marmalade
>Lake Superior Trout Meuniere
>Maple Poached Pears (Maple Glazed Pears)

(continued)

Old Rittenhouse Inn
Published Recipes

Marialisa Calta, "Whitefish Livers a Favorite for Years", *New York Times,*
7 February, 1990, n.p.
        Whitefish Livers

Linda and Fred Griffiths, *The Best of the Midwest,* (New York, Viking Penguin,
Studio Books, 1990)
        Crab Apple Jelly
        Pork Chops in Cream
        Salsa Cheesecake
        Snow Eggs in Red Raspberry Sauce
        Watercress Salad
        White Chocolate Muffins

Gail Greco, *Tea Time at the Inn,* (Tennesse, Rutledge Hill Press, 1991)
        Chocolate Mint Tea
        Lemon Cheesecake with Glazed Raspberries
        Orange Blossom Wedding Torte (Orange Blossom Torte)
        White Chocolate Muffins with Crabapple Jelly
        Wild Fruit Drop Scones with Blueberry Sauce (Wild Blueberry Scones)

Grace Howaniec, "No Mystery to Cranberries", Milwaukee Journal Magazine:
Milwaukee Journal, 24 November, 1991, n.p.
        Cranberry Sorbet (Cranberry Sherbet)

Ann Kaiser, "Country Inns + Farm Vacations", *Country,* December/January 1992
        Maple Walnut Pie

Suzy Taylor, "In a Snowbound Haven: A Valentine Feast", *Victoria,* February 1992
        Apple Glazed Pork Chops
        Strawberry Consommé
        White Chocolate Muffins

Meg Guthrie, *Best Recipes of Wisconsin Inns and Restaurants,*
(Wisconsin, Amherst Press, 1986)
        Maple Walnut Pie

Introduction

In 1973, a weathered Victorian mansion stood on the shores of Lake Superior in the beautiful town of Bayfield, Wisconsin. It was a relic of times past and, in many ways, forgotten. With innocence, naivety and a dream, a young couple entered the abandoned halls and rooms of this old house. Their enthusiasm for life left no room for the ghosts of the past. With their commitment, Mary and Jerry Phillips gave this place on earth a heartbeat, a soul, and a name . . . the Old Rittenhouse Inn.

Their dream is forged with honesty and integrity. A reverence for all people is interwoven with their love of music, cooking and fine craftsmanship. The Old Rittenhouse Inn has become a kaleidoscope of their talents and a reflection of the local community which has nurtured the Inn throughout the years. Because of their generous vitality, the Inn attracts others who share similar interests and desires. Each, in his or her own way, has added to the character of this place, making it more than an inn but rather a home. The Inn unites those who come here like family to partake in the pleasures of life: fine food, good music, friendship, and the hospitality of the Bayfield area.

The meals at the Inn begin with a savory presentation of a verbal menu which reflects the changing seasons. The selections provide the stage for the Inn's unique environment and leave guests with the memory of a delectable dining experience. From these dining experiences emerged certain recipes that are requested many times over.

This cookbook is a collection of those recipes, but it is not an end in itself. This book is part of a dynamic unfolding of a dream that has expanded to include inspirations, ideas and dreams of guests who have visited and revisited the Inn throughout the years.

We hope that when you prepare one of these selections, if you are a former guest, that you not only have a fine meal, but are also inspired to reflect back on an experience, a place in time, that brought joy to your life. If you have never been a guest at the Inn, then we welcome you to our dream and hope that any selection from this book will provide a back drop, again, not only to a fine meal, but also an occasion worth remembering.

As a member of the Old Rittenhouse Inn's staff, I am not a writer by trade. Innkeepers Mary and Jerry Phillips asked me to introduce this first and long awaited cookbook to you. I believe this request reflects the same sense of trust and belief that began the dream and continues to sustain it.

Mark McKenzie

Contents

Old Rittenhouse Inn

History

By creating a place that transcends time, we try to give our guests the same sense of well being and comfort we would extend to old friends. In so doing, we have made countless new friends, and the Old Rittenhouse Inn has grown and prospered.

It all started by falling in love—with a house, with a big lake, and with a small community that seemed comfortable with itself and in no hurry to be discovered. That was 1973. The house is a three-story Queen Anne which we offered to purchase by slipping a note under the front door. The lake is Longfellow's Gitche Gumee, Lake Superior, along Wisconsin's north coast. The town is Bayfield. Founded in 1856, it is built on a hillside overlooking a protected natural harbor.

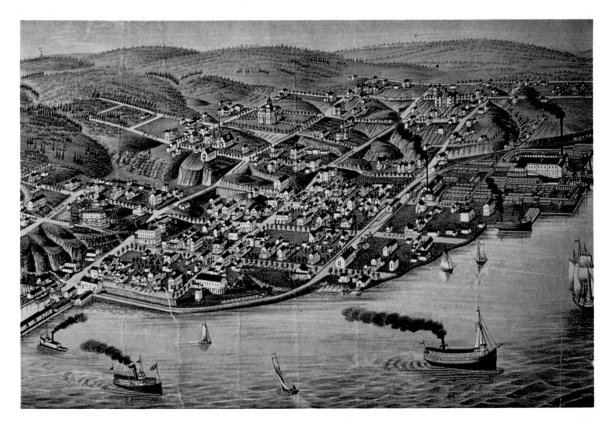

Bayfield isn't on the way to anywhere; unless you're looking for an archipelago of 22 islands, or the largest freshwater lake in the world. The National Park Service recognized the unique beauty of the area in 1970. The Apostle Islands National Lakeshore includes all but one of the islands surrounding the tip of the Bayfield peninsula as part of the park.

We spent our first two Bayfield summers transporting furniture from family attics. Hours spent at estate sales and auctions began to feed a growing passion for collecting antiques. But love met reality as the price of heating oil soared—and two music teachers' salaries stretched to cover a growing list of repairs and bills. With obvious room to spare, we occasionally were asked to take in overnight guests. We readily agreed.

Guests chose from five rooms. Each was furnished with antiques and a working fireplace, but all shared one bathroom in the hall. We offered to share our coffee, muffins, and summer fruit with these occasional guests. It wasn't long

before we became as interested in learning what brings travelers to Bayfield as they were in hearing about our plans for the house. Those first guests, who lingered over morning coffee, offering advice on everything from re-wiring antique light fixtures to restoring parquet flooring, inspired a business that was to become the Old Rittenhouse Inn. In them we found like-minded souls who traveled to meet new people, and to try new foods. They preferred a fireplace and conversation over a television (which we have resisted providing to this day).

We discussed the idea of becoming innkeepers. Perhaps we could show innkeeping as an economically viable way to give new life to an endangered species—the rambling Victorian mansion—too large for a single family dwelling, but architecturally irreplaceable. Bed & breakfast inns were becoming popular on the East Coast. But in the mid-1970s the concept took a lot of explaining in the Midwest. We decided it was worth a try. Leaving the security of city jobs behind,

we packed up our belongings, our four-year-old son, and moved north to Bayfield. That was 1976.

The slower pace of small town life was expected. But visiting a small town and trying to run a business in a remote area presented some surprises. It would be years before gasoline or groceries were available on Sundays. You planned ahead, borrowed, or you made do. Our survival became dependent on turning problems into new opportunities.

Fortunately, the Bayfield Peninsula's climate was long ago discovered to be ideally suited for growing fruit. Icy Lake Superior delays the arrival of blossoms in spring. In fall, the big lake's relative warmth holds off the frost until the fruit is harvested. Wild blueberries, fresh Lake Superior whitefish filets, and red raspberries (still warm from the sun in a neighbor's garden) appeared at our kitchen door more reliably than the wholesale delivery truck. Bushels of crisp red apples and apple blossom honey came from the orchards on the hill above town.

The availability of all these fresh ingredients inspired a frenzy of recipe testing and tasting. But it was impossible to execute all our ideas on a breakfast menu. It was time to expand the kitchen and offer guests the full range of Bayfield's bounty. Offering dinner demanded a division of responsibilities. Jerry baked breads and desserts, leaving him free to greet and serve. Mary took charge of the cooking. Our course was charted; local foods, creatively prepared to their best advantage became our goal.

The first dinner guests arrived on time, but the printed menus did not. Instructions from the kitchen were clear: "Just tell them what the choices are." The concept worked so well that when the menus arrived they were put on the shelf and never used. The verbal menu had become a tradition at the Inn. Far from being an inconvenience, verbal descriptions offer the flexibility to create menus that take full advantage of fresh fruits and vegetables in season. Explanation and encouragement are often needed when diners encounter local specialties such as sautéed whitefish livers or smoked trout salad for the first time.

Diners are always assured of a variety, but knowing that the menu will have a surprise or two becomes half the fun. Behind the scenes, the suspense is

balanced by the staff's careful review of the night's guest list to make sure someone's well-known favorite is among the night's choices.

We discovered other resources, though not large in number, were close at hand. They were our neighbors and new friends who shared their talents and became part of the Inn. Explaining our goals and philosophy to a mostly part-time, highly seasonal, and ever-changing staff comes only through hours of discussion in and around daily tasks. But it is time well spent. In turn staff

members have made countless contributions to the Inn. Some have left tangible evidence of their work; the ten-foot walnut headboard, a project of a former waiter, is a point of conversation for every tour of the Inn. Stained glass windows, carefully designed to compliment the foyer's cherry staircase is the work of an artist and friend. Housekeepers, talented in needlework, designed doilies and lace trim for china cabinet shelves. Handmade baskets and holiday ornaments are seasonal reminders of all who have helped to make the Inn feel like home.

Fitting into the fabric of a town of 700 takes time. And it's definitely not for everyone. It's two hours to the closest shopping mall, and 25 miles to a fast-food french fry. Acquaintances come easily, but friendships evolve more slowly and are built on trust—trust that you have come not only to reap the pleasures of the present, but that you plan to be part of the town's future.

So who are these people? They are the first people, the Native Americans who came to Madeline Island hundreds of years ago and later moved to the mainland.

They are the descendants of the French fur-trading voyagers and of loggers who clear cut the peninsula around the turn of the century. They are the occasional visitors who have decided to change lifestyles, and sometimes careers, to make Bayfield their home. And finally, there are the few who came for the weekend and couldn't bear to leave.

"Almost everyone who lives here," one writer observed, "seems to do so by choice." In a world where corporate transfers and career positioning decide where many call home, few people feel free to choose a community because it calls their name. An older resident was asked recently, "Have you lived in Bayfield all your life?" "No," she replied, "not yet."

Living in a small town also brings with it a certain responsibility. Individuals can greatly influence the future of the community if they are willing to get involved. The local historical society has taken an active role in safe guarding the town's history. In 1981, on Bayfield's 125th anniversary, the community's pride in its

heritage was recognized when a 50-block area was designated a historic district on the National Register of Historic Places. Bayfield's architectural treasurers have been restored one-by-one through local efforts. The waterfront pavilion and the old iron bridge have been taken on as projects. The most ambitious project transformed the old county courthouse from a storage building into the visitor's center for the Apostle Islands National Lakeshore.

Three of the historic district's significant structures have become part of the Old Rittenhouse Inn. Each has its own story to tell. The Inn itself was completed in 1892 as a summer home by Civil War General Allen C. Fuller and his wife Mary. The Fullers spent several summers in Bayfield, partly to relieve the General's hay fever. Perched on a knoll, the house overlooks Rittenhouse Avenue, the town's main street. The first floor parlor and sitting rooms serve as the Inn's dining rooms. Each room has a distinctive working fireplace, as do all the guest rooms.

The next member of the Inn's family is just four blocks away. Having lost a bid to purchase the home in the early 1970s, a second opportunity was irresistible. It is another Queen Anne-style mansion, complete with a turret and formal gardens. Frank Boutin, Jr., successful in lumbering and fishing operations, spared no expense in constructing this residence for his family in 1908. But stained glass windows, quarter-sawn oak paneling, and a wrap around porch with a commanding view of Lake Superior weren't enough to keep Mrs. Boutin from longing for big city life. After occupying the house for a short time, they moved on. Used alternately as a convent and a private residence, it became Le Chateau Boutin in 1985. The rose garden and restored fountain have been the site for many a summer wedding.

In 1986, Grey Oak Guest House was purchased and furnished in partnership with one of our staff. Only a short walk from the Inn, it was considered the outskirts of Bayfield when the home was built in 1888. The original owner, Ervin Leighy, was convinced the new town would prosper, and showed his confidence

by constructing a full basement of locally quarried brownstone. It was given its name to honor one of three massive trees that shade the porch: a Hickory, American Chestnut and a Grey Oak.

The logistics of running one business on three sites presented a challenge. How could we make all of our guests, no matter where they stay, feel a part of the Inn? The answer brought us back to where we started, to breakfast. While guests may choose to stay in the Turret Suite at Le Chateau Boutin or a cozy room at Grey Oak Guest House, everyone begins their day with breakfast at the Old Rittenhouse Inn. Over hot cranberry muffins topped with apple cider marmalade, guests can seek the staff's advice on their options for the day. "Should we take our car on the ferry to Madeline Island?" "Are any of the orchards selling apples this time of year?" "I read about the 'singing sand' on Stockton Island. Does the cruise boat take us there?" Conversations flow easily between tables as guests share experiences with each other. When the last sip of coffee is finished, they depart ready for adventure.

Browsing in the shops, day sailing, exploring Madeline Island or taking the day cruise among the islands are the readily apparent options. Registering for an a National Park Service lecture on eagle nesting in the area tend to be more easily overlooked. Since 1986, evening entertainment in the summer has been enhanced by Lake Superior Big Top Chautauqua. Combining local and national talent, Chautauqua offers three months of lectures, concerts, and a series of historical musicals that bring local history to life. Our challenge becomes making sure guests leave for home not only with memories, but with a list of things they want to do on their next visit.

Then there's winter. Bayfield's winter is a five-month season that stretches from the first November snow through the "isn't-it-spring-yet?" days of April. "What does everyone do here in the winter?" we're frequently asked. Some people choose to leave; some people just hibernate. Others see long winter evenings as an opportunity to indulge in hobbies, to catch up on reading, or to spend time with friends. Local residents note the season's progress by watching the lake. It freezes slowly until the ferry makes its last trip to Madeline Island about mid-January. Two months later speculation starts on when the first ferry will run.

At the Old Rittenhouse Inn, winter has come to mean holiday dinner concerts, mystery dinners, innkeeping seminars, and theater rehearsals. It wasn't always so busy. Our first Bayfield Christmas was quiet. It was too quiet. The hectic schedule of performing in city concerts and recitals was not missed, but we needed to bring music into the Inn. A call went out and the voices that responded became the Rittenhouse Chamber Singers. Now when the first leaves turn red, rehearsals begin. The combined musical talents of those who by day serve as lawyer, carpenter, beekeeper, and band director, are blended together and put into performance polish under Jerry's direction. Singers perform music to accompany holiday menus. The dinner concert season begins with Harvest in late October and continues through Christmas Wassail and Valentine's Day.

Several years ago another winter pastime was added. We started writing our own who-done-it mystery scripts. Staff members share clues with guests, and together they solve the "crime" over dinner. Many hidden theatrical talents are discovered during these evenings of fun and entertainment.

We took a big risk when we traded two promising careers in music for life in Northern Wisconsin. Starting an inn with no formal training in business or cooking isn't a course we'd recommend for anyone. But as we look back, the Inn

has provided the perfect opportunity to combine our interests in meeting people, cooking, music, theater and historic preservation into a business of our own. The adventure continues as we share our first cookbook with you.

We shall not cease from exploration
And the end of all our exploring
Will be to arrive where we started
And to know the place for the first time.
T.S. Elliott

Old Rittenhouse Inn

Appetizers

Whitefish Liver Paté

6 servings

2 pounds whitefish livers, rinsed, drained, and patted dry
6 tablespoons butter
2 garlic cloves
1 teaspoon salt
½ teaspoon ground black pepper
¼ teaspoon ground allspice
½ teaspoon ground nutmeg
2 tablespoons cognac
1 teaspoon lemon juice

Trout, cod or sole livers may be substituted.

1. Heat butter in a skillet until it bubbles. Sauté livers over medium heat until brown on the outside. Remove from heat. Drain off excess butter.
2. Combine garlic, seasonings, cognac, lemon juice and livers in a food processor fitted with a steel blade. Process until smooth and creamy.
3. Transfer paté to a crock. Cover and refrigerate at least 4 hours. Let stand 30 minutes at room temperature before serving.

Spinach Crêpes

with Golden Caviar

12-14 small crêpes

Crêpes—

¼ pound fresh spinach
1 cup flour
1 egg
2 cups milk
Oil for frying crêpes

Filling—

½ cup softened cream cheese
½ cup sour cream
½ cup grated mozzarella cheese
¼ cup chopped chives
½ cup golden caviar

Hollandaise—

(see recipe on page 106)

Garnish—

Caviar
Fresh lime or lemon

CRÊPES

1. Temper your crêpe pan by warming on low heat with 2 tablespoons of vegetable oil for 30 minutes.
2. Purée spinach in food processor fitted with steel blade.
3. Add flour, egg, and milk to spinach. Process until well blended.
4. Fry crêpes, using 2-3 tablespoons of batter for each. With deft turning of the pan as you pour in the batter, and with the back of a spoon to help, you can produce nice, thin crêpes.

FILLING

1. Saving the caviar until last, mix the filling ingredients and blend until smooth.
2. Put 2 tablespoons of filling in each crêpe and roll up.
3. Top with hollandaise, garnish, and serve immediately.

Stuffed Mushrooms

6 servings

12 large mushrooms
3 tablespoons olive oil
2 garlic cloves, peeled and
   minced
¼ cup green onions, finely
   chopped
¼ cup grated parmesan cheese
¼ cup grated cheddar cheese
¼ cup sour cream
¼ cup toasted bread crumbs
2 teaspoons chopped parsley
1 teaspoon chopped basil
Salt and pepper to taste
2 tablespoons butter

1. Preheat oven to 300 degrees
2. Remove stems from mushroom caps. Set caps aside and chop the stems finely.
3. Heat oil in frying pan. Add garlic, onions, and chopped mushroom stems. Sauté while stirring, for 3 minutes.
4. Remove from heat. Mix in remaining ingredients, except butter.
5. Place mushroom caps in a baking dish. Fill each with mixture. Put a bit of butter on each cap. Bake at 300 degrees for 10 minutes, or until golden brown.

Salsa Cheesecake

one 9-inch cheesecake

2 tablespoons melted butter
½ cup very fine bread crumbs
¾ pound cream cheese
¼ pound roquefort cheese
1 cup sour cream
2 tablespoons flour
1 cup grated parmesan cheese
½ cup salsa
4 large eggs

Garnish—

Leaves of fresh kale
Fresh cilantro
Minced cilantro
Minced parsley

1. Preheat the oven to 350 degrees. Brush sides and bottom of a 9-inch springform pan with the melted butter and carefully coat with ¼ cup bread crumbs. Tap out excess.
2. In the bowl of an electric mixer, combine the cream cheese and roquefort. Add sour cream, flour, parmesan, and salsa, beating well between additions. Scrape bowl, turn motor to high, and add eggs one at a time. Scrape bowl and beat well to make certain all is blended properly. Pour batter into pre-pared pan. Sprinkle with remaining bread crumbs.
3. Carefully wrap bottom of pan in foil and set in a larger baking dish filled with hot water. Or place pan in oven over another filled with hot water. (Cake will be a bit higher if baked in a water bath.) Bake 1¼ hours. Cool in oven, with door ajar, 1 hour.
4. Place 1 or 2 leaves of fresh kale on each serving plate. Top with a slice of cheesecake. Then garnish plate with cilantro and sprinkle with minced cilantro and parsley. Serve warm or at room temperature.

Deviled Eggs

8 servings

8 hard boiled eggs
1 teaspoon anchovy paste
¼ cup mayonnaise
1 teaspoon lemon juice
1 clove fresh garlic, minced
½ teaspoon onion, minced
½ teaspoon dijon-style mustard
Dash of hot pepper sauce
Salt and pepper to taste

Garnish—

Paprika
Black olives, sliced

1. Slice the eggs in half lengthwise. Remove yolks and mash them in a mixing bowl.
2. Add anchovy paste, mayonnaise and lemon juice. Mix until smooth.
3. Stir in garlic, onion, mustard, hot pepper sauce, salt and pepper.
4. Fill egg white halves with the mixture.
5. Garnish with paprika and black olives. Chill until ready to serve.

Seviche Superior

6 servings

½ pound fresh lake trout fillets
½ pound fresh whitefish fillets
¾ cup fresh lime juice
¼ cup fresh lemon juice
½ teaspoon salt
¼ cup chopped onion
¼ cup chopped green bell
   pepper
2 tablespoons minced fresh dill
   weed
½ teaspoon minced fresh garlic
¼ teaspoon cracked pepper, or
3-4 drops hot pepper sauce

*For a real treat, serve garnished
with whitefish caviar.*

1. Skin trout and whitefish and cut into bite-sized pieces.
2. In a glass or stainless steel bowl combine fish with lime and lemon juice and salt. Stir until salt is dissolved.
3. Add the rest of the ingredients and stir well to mix.
4. Cover and refrigerate for 24 hours, stirring several times.
5. Remove from brine and serve, or may be stored tightly covered for several days.

Old Rittenhouse Inn

Soups

Red Raspberry Soup

4-6 servings

1 pound chopped rhubarb
4 cups raspberries
¾ cup sugar
1 three-inch cinnamon stick
2 cups water
½ cup red Burgundy wine
½ cup well chilled club soda

Garnish—

Fresh mint leaf

1. Combine rhubarb, two cups of raspberries, sugar, cinnamon stick, and water. Bring the mixture to a boil. Stir and simmer for 5 minutes, or until the rhubarb is tender.
2. Strain the mixture into a bowl.
3. Stir Burgundy wine into the juice. Chill for two hours.
4. Just before serving, stir in the remaining two cups of red raspberries, and the club soda.
5. Garnish.

Apple Cider Cream Soup

8 servings

Cream—

1 quart apple cider (apple juice
    may be substituted)
½ cup orange juice concentrate
1 stick cinnamon
Grated peel of 1 medium lemon
½ cup cornstarch
1¼ cups Gewurztraminer wine
    or sparkling grape juice
¼ cup brown sugar
½ cup whipping cream
1 cup slivered apples, unpeeled

Garnish—

Whipped cream
Chopped walnuts

1. Mix cider, orange juice, cinnamon stick, and lemon peel. Bring to a boil, reduce heat and simmer for 5 minutes. Remove cinnamon stick.
2. In a small bowl, blend cornstarch and wine to form a smooth paste. Add paste to cider mixture. Cook over low heat until soup is thickened and smooth, stirring continually.
3. Add sugar and whipping cream. Remove from heat. Fold in slivered apples.
4. Serve hot or chilled, garnished with a dollop of whipped cream and chopped walnuts.

Strawberry Consommé

8 servings

2 cups strawberry juice
2 cups cranberry juice
1 cup apple juice
¾ cup sugar
⅛ teaspoon ground cardamom
⅛ teaspoon ground coriander
½ cup dry red wine
½ cup club soda
1 pint fresh strawberries,
   stemmed and sliced

Garnish—

Sliced strawberries
Fresh mint leaves

May be served hot or chilled.

Note: It's very easy to make strawberry juice. Simply bring 1 quart of crushed fresh berries to boil in a saucepan with 2 cups of cold water. Reduce heat and simmer for 30 minutes. Strain strawberry pulp, return juice to sauce pan, and reduce to 2 cups liquid. Chill or serve warm.

1. Combine strawberry juice, cranberry juice, apple juice, sugar, cardamom and coriander. Bring to boil.
2. Remove from heat. Stir in red wine.
3. Just before serving, add club soda. Garnish with sliced, stemmed strawberries and mint leaves.

Cream of Almond Soup

8 servings

Soup—

6 cups chicken stock
1 cup cooked, finely chopped breast of chicken
2 cups slightly undercooked wild rice
1 tablespoon lemon juice
¼ teaspoon almond extract
1 cup slivered almonds
1 cup heavy cream

Garnish—

1 cup grated cheddar or swiss cheese

1. Bring stock to a boil. Reduce heat and simmer gently for five minutes.
2. Add chicken, wild rice, lemon juice and almond extract.
3. Just before serving, add almonds and cream.
4. Garnish with grated cheese.

Curried Broccoli Soup

6-8 servings

1 ½ pounds broccoli (3 average stalks)
2 cups chicken stock or broth
3-4 cloves garlic (good sized) minced
¼ cup minced green onions— tops included
½ teaspoon nutmeg
¾ teaspoon curry
1 cup heavy cream

Garnish—

Broccoli flowerettes

1. Cut off heads (flowerettes) of brocolli, wash and set aside.
2. Peel the stalks—mince or run through food processor in several bursts.
3. Place broccoli puree, stock, garlic and onion in saucepan—bring to a boil, lower and simmer uncovered for 15 minutes.
4. Place in food processor and blend until smooth.
5. Return to sauce pan and simmer on low heat.
6. Add nutmeg, curry, and heavy cream. Warm and serve.
7. Garnish with the remaining broccoli flowerettes.

Pumpkin Soup

with Hazelnut Cream

6 servings

Soup—

2 cups peeled, seeded, cooked
    pumpkin, fresh or canned
¼ cup chopped onion
2 tablespoons melted butter
½ cup dry sherry
4 cups chicken stock
¼ cup maple syrup
½ teaspoon curry
½ teaspoon ground mace
½ teaspoon minced fresh sage
¼ teaspoon ground cumin

Hazelnut Cream—

2 ounces shelled and roasted
    hazelnuts, finely chopped
1 teaspoon hazelnut liqueur or
    several drops of hazelnut oil
½ cup heavy cream, whipped or
    ½ cup sour cream

Garnishes—

Dill sprigs and nasturtium or
    violet petals

*Walnuts and walnut oil may be
substituted.*

SOUP
1. In processor fitted with steel blade, blend pumpkin until smooth.
2. Sauté onion in butter until opaque in small pan.
3. Add onion, butter, sherry, stock, syrup and seasonings to pumpkin and process until creamy and smooth.

CREAM
1. In a small bowl, fold nuts and liqueur or oil into whipped cream.
2 To serve, ladle soup into bowls. Top with hazelnut cream, and garnish each bowl with a sprig of dill and edible flowers.

Avocado Vichyssoise

6 servings

Soup—

2 cups yogurt
2 cups puréed avocado
1 cup chicken stock
2 cups heavy cream
1 tablespoon minced fresh
    fennel
1 teaspoon minced fresh sage
⅛ teasoon ground coriander

Garnish—

Chopped onion
Dill
Sour Cream

1. In a blender, or a food processor fitted with a steel blade, blend yogurt, avocado, chicken stock, and cream. Mix in seasonings.
2. Chill.
3. Serve in chilled bowls.
4. Garnish with chopped onions, dill and a dollop of sour cream.

Roquefort Vichyssoise

6 servings

Vichyssoise—

1 cup finely chopped leek
½ cup finely chopped onion
¼ cup butter
1 quart chicken stock
2 cups uncooked hash browns
¾ cup roquefort cheese
2 cups heavy whipping cream
Salt and pepper to taste

Garnish—

2 tablespoons chopped parsley
2 tablespoons chopped chives

Note: Wild leeks give this recipe a special flavor. Simply substitute 1½ cups of wild leeks for the onions and regular leeks.

1. Sauté leek and onion in butter over low heat.
2. Add chicken stock and potatoes. Simmer until potatoes are cooked.
3. Pureé in food processor fitted with steel blade until smooth.
4. Remove from processor and put in non-aluminum container. Stir in roquefort and cream. Add salt and pepper to taste.
5. Serve hot or cold. Garnish with chopped parsley and chives.

Whitefish Chowder

6-8 servings

½ cup chopped onions
½ cup chopped wild leek
2 tablespoons butter
2½ cups uncooked hash
  browns
2 cups chopped clams
3 cups clam juice
1 cup whole kernel corn
⅓ cup minced parsley
1 tablespoon minced fresh
  dill weed
1 tablespoon minced fresh basil
½ teaspoon minced fresh fennel
1 teaspoon cracked pepper
2 pounds cooked whitefish, skin
  removed, cut into pieces
1 cup slightly undercooked wild
  rice
1½ cup heavy whipping cream
1 cup milk
6 slices bacon, fried and broken

Garnish—

Parsley
Paprika

1. Sauté onions and leeks in butter over low heat until tender.
2. Add hash browns, clams, clam juice, corn and seasonings and bring to a boil. Reduce heat to low.
3. Add whitefish, wild rice, whipping cream, milk and bacon. Heat through, and serve garnished with chopped parsley and paprika.

Whitefish Bisque

with Shiitake Mushrooms

8 servings

Soup—

¼ teaspoon powdered saffron
1 cup heavy cream
½ pound stemmed and sliced shiitake mushroom caps
½ cup chopped green onions, whites only
3 tablespoons butter
1 cup fish stock (see recipe on page 139)
1 pound cooked, flaked white-fish with skin removed
1 tablespoon fresh lemon juice
3 egg yolks
2 cups milk
Salt
White pepper
Ground cayenne pepper

Garnish—

Sour cream
¼ cup chopped red bell pepper
1 tablespoon minced dill weed
Paprika

1. In a small bowl, stir the saffron into the cream and set aside to flavor.
2. Sauté the mushrooms and onion in the butter on medium heat.
3. Add stock and whitefish. Cook until fish falls apart, about 10-15 minutes
4. Transfer to a food processor fitted with a steel blade or blender and purée until very smooth and creamy.
5. Whisk the lemon juice, yolks and milk into the saffron cream. Add about ¼ cup of the whitefish mixture and blend.
6. Return this mixture to the food processor and blend.
7. Transfer to saucepan and warm on low heat until just below the boiling point. Season with salt, pepper and cayenne to taste.
8. Garnish and serve.

Tomato Tortilla Soup

8 servings

Soup—

4 cups tomato sauce
4 cups chopped tomatoes
¼ cup chicken stock
½ cup chopped onions
½ cup chopped green peppers
½ cup hot salsa
2-3 cloves minced garlic

Garnish—

Sour cream
Tortilla chips
Cheddar cheese, shredded

1. Combine all ingredients in a medium size sauce pan. Bring to a boil, reduce heat, and simmer for 10 minutes.
2. Place large tortilla chips around inside of the soup bowl, so they appear to be forming a taco shell for the soup in the middle. Garnish with sour cream, tortilla chips, and shredded cheddar cheese. (Colby or monterey jack may be substituted.)

Snow White Chili

8 servings

Soup—

2 cups white navy or white lima beans
6 cups chicken or turkey stock
4 minced garlic cloves
2 pounds boneless cooked turkey breast, chopped
1 cup chopped white onion
¼ teaspoon ground cumin
½ teaspoon curry
1 teaspoon white pepper
1 teaspoon salt
½ teaspoon crushed red hot pepper
16 ounces sweet corn, white if possible
8 ounces heavy cream

Garnish—

Monteray jack cheese
Chopped scallions
Chopped cilantro
Chopped bell pepper, red and/or green
Tortilla chips

SOUP

1. In a large saucepan, combine beans and stock. Let sit overnight.
2. Cook beans in stock with garlic until tender but not soft.
3. Add turkey, onion, seasonings and corn. Simmer for 15 minutes. Taste and correct seasoning if desired.
4. Just before serving, add cream, and heat through.
5. Garnish each bowl with shredded monterey jack cheese, chopped scallions, chopped cilantro, chopped red or green peppers and tortilla chips.

Old Rittenhouse Inn

Salads

Smoked Trout Salad

with Almond Toast

6-8 servings

Smoked Trout Salad—

2 cups fresh spinach, broken
2 cups red lettuce, broken
2 cups romaine lettuce, broken
18 ounces smoked trout, flaked
1 cup slivered almonds

Vinagrette Dressing—

½ cup lemon juice
¼ cup orange juice concentrate
1 tablespoon white wine vinegar
1 tablespoon dijon-style mustard
¾ cup mayonnaise
Salt and white pepper to taste
1½ tablespoons minced shallots
2 tablespoons chopped cilantro
1 cup diced tomatoes

Almond Toast—

3 ounces butter, softened
1 tablespoon finely chopped
    fresh basil
1 cup slivered almonds
12 slices French bread, sliced
    1½ inches thick on a bias

Garnish—

6-8 fresh edible flowers

SALAD

1. Toss the greens together and place on chilled plates.
2. Place flaked trout on greens.
3. Sprinkle with almonds.
4. Drizzle with dressing.
5. Garnish with a fresh, edible flower.
6. Serve with almond toast.

VINAGRETTE DRESSING

1. Blend first five ingredients in food processor.
2. Salt and pepper to taste.
3. Place in medium sauce pan. Stir in the shallots, cilantro and tomatoes.
4. Heat just to boiling point. Remove from heat.

ALMOND TOAST

1. Process butter, basil, almonds in a food processor until the mixture is creamy.
2. Coat the bread on each side with almond butter.
3. Wrap in foil and heat in 350 degree oven for 10-15 minures. Open foil and brown for 5 minutes. Keep warm.

Bayfield Smoked Herring Salad

8 servings

Salad—

4 cups smoked herring, boned and flaked (smoked trout or whitefish may be substituted)
½ cup hash browns, crisply cooked and chilled
1 cup grated cheddar cheese
½ cup grated swiss cheese
2 tablespoons sliced green olives, pitted
½ cup red bell pepper, seeded and chopped
1 teaspoon white pepper
1 cup chopped chives

Dressing—

1 cup heavy cream, whipped
3 tablespoons lemon juice
2 teaspoons dark, dijon-style, mustard
2 teaspoons anchovy paste
1 cup mayonnaise

1 tablespoon fresh dill weed, chopped

Garnishes—

Lemon wedges
Cooked, chopped beets, chilled and drained
Chopped hard boiled eggs, chilled

SALAD
1. Toss all ingredients together. Keep well chilled.

DRESSING
1. Blend all ingredients until smooth. Pour over salad, toss and garnish.

GARNISHES
Any or all of these garnishes may be served on the side of the salad.

Asparagus Salad

with Sesame Seeds

6 servings

Salad—

1 pound Bibb lettuce, chilled
10 ounces cooked asparagus,
    cut into 1½ inch pieces
½ cup sliced red radishes
½ cup minced red onion

Dressing—

¼ cup white wine vinegar
¼ cup chicken broth
1 tablespoon soy sauce
2 teaspoons sugar
3 tablespoons olive oil
1 teaspoon sesame oil
2 teaspoons peeled and grated
    ginger root

Garnish—

¾ cup toasted sesame seeds

SALAD
1. Toss together all ingredients and chill.

DRESSING
1. Combine vinegar, broth, soy sauce, and sugar.
2. Add oils.
3. Stir in ginger root.
4. Pour dressing over salad, toss and garnish with sesame seeds.

Asparagus Salad

with Spinach Vinaigrette

6 servings

6 beautiful lettuce leaves
24 spears asparagus, cooked al
   dente (still firm to the bite)
⅛ cup chopped capers
⅛ cup chopped chives
¼ cup slivered black olives
⅛ cup chopped parsley
1 cup spinach dressing (see
   recipe on page 52)

For each serving:
1. On a lettuce leaf, arrange 4 asparagus
   spears. Drizzle ⅙ cup dressing over
   asparagus.
2. Sprinkle ⅙ of the capers, chives, olives, and
   parsley over top of each salad.

Spinach Salad

6-8 servings

Salad—

1 pound fresh spinach, washed and drained
8 ounces chopped or sliced water chestnuts
1 cup slivered mushrooms
½ pound bacon, crisply fried and crumbled
3 hard boiled eggs, sliced
1 large mild red onion, thinly sliced

Dressing—

1 cup salad oil
¾ cup sugar
½ cup lemon juice
½ cup mild salsa
⅛ teaspoon grated nutmeg

Shiitake mushrooms are especially good with spinach.

SALAD
1. Toss spinach, water chestnuts, and mushrooms. Place on chilled salad plates.
2. On each salad, arrange bacon, eggs, and red onion.

DRESSING
1. Blend all ingredients and chill.
2. Pour dressing over salad just before serving, and pass the pepper mill.

Watercress Salad

6 servings

1 head romaine lettuce, washed, dried, and torn into bite-size pieces
Fresh tomatoes sliced
1 cucumber, cut in julienne strips
1 zucchini, cut in julienne strips
1 green bell pepper, finely chopped
6 scallions, finely chopped
2 bunches fresh watercress, drained, tough stems removed
Vinaigrette of your choice
Salt and freshly ground black pepper to taste

1. Place romaine on chilled salad plates and arrange 3 slices of tomato, slightly overlapping, in the center of the romaine.
2. Top the tomatoes with alternating strips of cucumber and zucchini.
3. Sprinkle with chopped green pepper and scallions. Surround the vegetables with the watercress.
4. Dress with vinaigrette, salt, and freshly ground pepper.

Sour Cream Potato Salad

6 servings

Salad—

4 cups chilled, diced, cooked potatoes
1½ cups diced cucumbers
½ cup thinly sliced radishes
2 tablespoons chopped green onions
½ teaspoon salt
¼ teaspoon ground white pepper
½ teaspoon minced garlic
¼ pound cooked bacon-extra crispy
3 hard boiled egg whites, diced

Dressing—

3 hard boiled egg yolks
½ cup mayonnaise
½ cup sour cream
¼ cup white vinegar
Sugar to taste

SALAD
1. Mix together potatoes, cucumbers, radishes, onion, salt, pepper, garlic, and crispy bacon.
2. Add diced egg whites to potato mixture.

DRESSING
1. Mash yolks. Combine with mayonnaise, sour cream, and vinegar. Mix thoroughly.
2. Just before serving, lightly toss the dressing with the salad, and sweeten to taste with sugar.

Wisconsin Farmhouse Salad

with Molasses-Bacon Dressing

8 servings

Salad—

4 cups fresh spinach
2 cups wild rice, cooked and chilled
40 one inch boneless pork strips, cooked and chilled
8 new red potatoes, boiled with skins on, and chilled
1 cup sliced mushrooms
¼ cup chopped red onions
¼ cup grated carrot
8 cherry tomatoes, split almost through

Molasses-Bacon Dressing—

5 cloves garlic, peeled
1 cup chopped sweet onion (average medium onion)
⅛ cup fresh basil
¾ cup red wine vinegar
½ cup olive oil
1 cup molasses
1 cup honey
½ pound bacon, fried crispy

SALAD

For each salad:
1. Make a bed of ½ cup spinach on a chilled plate.
2. Place ¼ cup cooked wild rice on spinach.
3. Arrange 5 pieces of pork in an arc.
4. Form another arc underneath with 5 slices of boiled potato.
5. Arrange ⅛ cup sliced mushrooms.
6. Sprinkle onion and carrot over potatoes for color.
7. Place a split tomato on the side.

DRESSING

1. Combine all ingredients except bacon, and process 10 seconds in processor.
2. Drizzle dressing over the salad, or serve in a separate bowl. There may be extra dressing for another time.
3. Crumble the bacon over salad.

Harlequin Bean Salad

with Garlic Sauce

6-8 servings

Salad—

6 cups chicken stock
1 cup small white beans
1 cup black beans

Sauce—

3 tablespoons finely chopped
   garlic
3 teaspoons lemon juice
¼ cup olive oil
2 tablespoons chopped green
   onion
2 tablespoons of chopped fresh
   cilentro
10 ounces fresh spinach leaves

Garnish—

Chopped crisp bacon
Crumbled feta cheese

SALAD
1. Put each type of bean in a separate sauce pan with 3 cups of stock, cover and simmer until just tender. (Each type requres different cooking times.)
2. Rinse in cold water and drain well. Chill.

SAUCE
1. Combine ingredients except spinach leaves.
2. Add chilled beans.
3. Place spinach on chilled plates. Top with ½ cup of bean mixture.
4. Garnish with bacon and feta cheese.

Lentil Salad

6-8 servings

2 cups dry lentils (half green/
 half red)
5 cups chicken stock
1 small red onion, chopped
1 jalapeno pepper, chopped
2 tablespoons chopped cilantro
6 cloves minced garlic
½ cup olive oil
1 teaspoon salt
½ teaspoon coarsely ground
 pepper
24 green pimento stuffed olives,
 sliced
2 tablespoons fresh lemon juice
1 cup sliced fresh mushrooms

*This salad is delicious served
with avocado slices or vine
ripened tomatoes.*

1. Cook lentils in chicken stock until done, but al dente (still firm to the bite).
2. Drain excess liquid and chill.
3. Combine all other ingredients.
4. Mix cooled lentils and other ingredients. Cover and marinate overnight in the refrigerator.

Old Rittenhouse Inn

Dressings

Rittenhouse Yogurt Dressing

2¾ cups

2 cups vanilla or lemon yogurt
½ cup strawberry or red raspberry jelly
¼ cup honey
¼ teaspoon of nutmeg

1. Blend all ingredients until smooth.
2. Chill in a covered container. This is excellent served with fresh fruit.

Chutney Dressing

1¼ cups

¾ cup olive oil
¼ cup lemon juice
¼ cup cranberry chutney (see
   recipe on page 92)
1 teaspoon curry powder
½ teaspoon ground pepper

1. Blend all ingredients.
2. Cover and chill at least 4 hours before serving.

Herbed Cheese Dressing

3½ cups

1 cup grated sharp cheddar
   cheese
½ cup feta cheese
1 cup mayonnaise
1 cup chopped parsley
4 tablespoons lemon juice
1 tablespoon soy sauce
2 cloves minced garlic
2 teaspoons ground basil
½ cup chopped chives

1. In a blender or a food processor fitted with a steel blade, blend all ingredients, except chives, until creamy and smooth.
2. Fold in chives. Chill before serving.

Blue Cheese Dressing

2½ cups

2 cups mayonnaise
6 tablespoons heavy cream
4 tablespoons lemon juice
2 tablespoons finely chopped
   onion
4 teaspoons sugar
1 teaspoon soy sauce
1 teaspoon Worcestershire
   sauce
½ teaspoon dry mustard
8 ounces crumbled blue cheese

1. Blend all ingredients, except blue cheese, until smooth and creamy.
2. Fold in blue cheese. Chill before serving.

French Cream Dressing

2½ cups

2 cups mayonnaise
2 tablespoons lemon juice
2 tablespoons lime juice
¼ cup sugar
2 tablespoons heavy cream
2 teaspoons paprika
1 teaspoon Rittenhouse
   Reddening (see recipe on
   page 96)

1. Blend all ingredients well.
2. Chill before serving.

Red Wine Vinaigrette

2 cups

½ cup red wine vinegar
2 cloves garlic
3 teaspoons dry mustard
1 cup olive oil
¼ cup red onion
½ cup black pitted olives

1. Process in food processor.
2. Store in a covered container.

Old Rittenhouse Inn

Breads

Wild Rice Bread

2 loaves

½ cup buttermilk (110-115 degrees)

2 tablespoons yeast, dry active

2 tablespoons honey (110 degrees)

1 tablespoon salt

2 cups well cooked wild rice, well drained

3 cups all-purpose flour

½ cup melted butter

½ cup warm honey

2 eggs, room temperature

½ cup warm buttermilk

1 ½ cups flour, to finish bread

1. Proof yeast in buttermilk with honey.
2. Combine salt, wild rice, and flour in processor, fitted with a steel blade. Blend until rice is finely processed.
3. Transfer rice mixture to a large mixing bowl.
4. Add proofed yeast to wild rice mixture. Add butter, honey, eggs, and buttermilk.
5. Add enough of the flour to form dough. Turn out on floured board. Knead 5-10 minutes, or until dough is no longer sticky.
6. Place dough in a large buttered bowl. Lightly butter the top and cover. Let rise until double in size. Punch down and knead briefly. Cover and let rise for 30 minutes.
7. Place on floured board and divide in half. Form into large balls and let rest for 15 minutes.
8. Preheat oven to 350 degrees.
9. Shape into loaves and place in buttered loaf pans (8½ by 4½). Cover and let rise until double.
10. Bake at 350 degrees for 45 minutes, or until done.

English Muffin Bread

2 loaves or 18 rolls

2 tablespoons active dry yeast
½ cup warm water (115 degrees)
1 tablespoon honey
3 cups all purpose white flour
1 cup whole wheat flour
½ cup corn meal
1 tablespoon salt
2 cups warm milk
¼ cup warm honey
¾ to 1¼ cups flour to finish

1. Proof yeast in water with 1 tablespoon honey in small bowl.
2. Combine flours, corn meal and salt in large bowl.
3. Add milk, honey and yeast mixture to dry ingredient and beat for 5-10 minutes, or until a sticky batter is formed.
4. Beating slowly, add enough flour to mixture to develop a soft dough.
5. Turn into a medium sized, greased bowl. Let rise until double in size and punch down.
6. Preheat oven to 325 degrees and grease pans.
7. Form into 2 loaves or 18 rolls. Put into pans. Let rise until double in size.
8. Bake until golden brown (30-35 minutes for loaves or 12-15 minutes for rolls.)

Black Pepper Bread

2 loaves

2 tablespoons active dry yeast
½ cup warm water (110-115
   degrees)
1 tablespoon honey
3 cups all purpose white flour
1 tablespoon salt
½ cup softened butter
1 cup warm buttermilk
1 egg
1 ½ to 2 cups all-purpose white
   flour
Warm water to form dough
2 tablespoons coarsely ground
   black pepper, or to taste
2 tablespoons crisp bacon
   pieces (3 slices)
2 tablespoons coarse sea salt

1. In a small bowl, proof yeast in water with honey.
2. In a large mixing bowl, with an electric mixer fitted with a paddle, combine 3 cups flour and salt.
3. In a separate bowl, combine butter, buttermilk, egg, and yeast mixture. Add to the flour and salt mixture. Beat 5 minutes at medium speed.
4. Change paddle to dough hook and continue adding enough flour to form a soft dough. Turn onto a floured board and knead. Place into large greased mixing bowl, grease top, and let rise until double in size.
5. Punch dough down. Turn back onto floured board. Divide in half and let dough rest 10 minutes.
6. Roll out each half into a rectangle approximately 8 inch x 14 inch with a rolling pin. Brush with warm water.
7. Sprinkle each rectangle with 1 tablespoon bacon and one tablespoon pepper. Roll into loaves, sealing each loaf with water. Put into greased loaf pans and let rise until double in size.
8. Preheat oven to 325 degrees.
9. Brush each loaf with warm water and top with sea salt.
10. Bake 30-35 minutes or until golden brown.

Cardamom Bread

2 loaves or 18 rolls

2 tablespoons active dry yeast
½ cup warm water (110-115 degrees)
1 tablespoon warm honey
4 cups all-purpose flour
1 teaspoon salt
2 teaspoons ground cardamom
½ cup melted butter
2 eggs, room temperature
1 cup warm milk
½ cup warm honey
1½ cups all-purpose flour

1. Proof yeast in water with honey.
2. Combine flour, salt, and cardamom in a large mixing bowl.
3. Combine butter, eggs, milk, and honey and add to dry ingredients. Fold in yeast mixture. Add enough flour to form a soft dough. Turn out on floured board, and knead until dough is no longer sticky. (5-10 minutes)
4. Place in a large buttered bowl, lightly butter top of dough, cover and let rise until double in size.
5. Punch dough down and knead briefly. Cover and let rest 15 minutes.
6. Preheat oven to 350 degrees and grease pans.
7. Form into 2 loaves; (or if you prefer rolls), lightly grease hands, squeeze dough through thumb and forefinger, producing a ball. Twist off and put in greased muffin tin. Let rise until double in size and bake at 350 degrees for 15 minutes for rolls or 35-45 minutes for loaves, until light brown.

Black Walnut Cheese Loaf

1 loaf

2 cups flour
2 teaspoons baking powder
1 teaspoon salt
1 cup grated swiss cheese
¼ cup chopped black walnuts
¼ cup fresh chopped chives
2 large eggs, lightly beaten
⅔ cup milk
⅓ cup vegetable oil

English Walnuts or pecans may be substituted.

1. Preheat oven to 350 degrees and grease a 4½ by 8½ inch bread pan.
2. In a large bowl, sift dry ingredients together. Add cheese, walnuts and chives.
3. Beat together eggs, milk and oil in a separate bowl. Add to the dry ingredients and mix.
4. Turn into greased bread pan. Bake 35 to 45 minutes or until toothpick inserted in center comes out clean.
5. Turn out onto wire rack to cool.

Apple Butter Bread

1 loaf

1 ½ cups all-purpose white flour
½ cup rolled oats
1 cup white sugar
1 teaspoon baking powder
½ teaspoon baking soda
1 teaspoon cinnamon
½ teaspoon ground ginger
½ teaspoon grated nutmeg
3 large eggs
¼ cup vegetable oil
¾ cup apple cider marmalade (optional) (see recipe on page 81)
¼ cup lemonade concentrate
½ cup milk
½ cup chopped walnuts
1 cup finely chopped apples
1 tablespoon grated lemon peel
1 tablespoon grated orange peel

Note: We find that glass baking pans give the best results for a high loaf without over-browning.

1. Preheat oven to 300-325 degrees. Grease and flour a 4½ inch x 8½ inch loaf pan.
2. In a large mixing bowl, mix flour, oats, sugar, baking powder, baking soda and spices.
3. In medium sized bowl, beat eggs, oil, apple cider marmalade, lemonade concentrate and milk.
4. Stir in walnuts, apples, lemon peel and orange peel.
5. Combine wet to dry ingredients.
6. Pour mixture into prepared pan. Bake 1 to 1¼ hours, or until a toothpick inserted in the center comes out clean.
7. Remove from pan and cool to room temperature.

Swiss Corn Muffins

12-18 muffins

1 ¼ cups cornmeal
1 ¼ cups all purpose white flour
¼ cup white sugar
6 teaspoons baking powder
¼ teaspoon ground white pepper
¼ teaspoon ground red cayenne pepper
¾ cup milk
½ cup bacon grease or vegetable oil
2 large eggs, lightly beaten
2 teaspoons minced garlic (2-3 cloves)
½ cup grated swiss cheese
½ cup chopped red or green bell pepper
½ cup grated carrot
½ cup sweet corn kernels, fresh or frozen

1. Preheat oven to 350 degrees and grease muffin tins.
2. Combine cornmeal, flour, sugar, baking powder, white pepper, and red pepper. Blend well.
3. In separate bowl combine milk, oil, and eggs.
4. Add wet ingredients to dry.
5. Fold in garlic, cheese, peppers, carrots, and sweet corn.
6. Pour batter into muffin tins, filling each ¾ full. Bake 10 minutes or until golden.

White Chocolate Muffins

12 large muffins

1 large egg
¼ cup vegetable oil
¾ cup white chocolate liquor
½ cup milk
½ teaspoon almond extract
2 cups flour
¼ cup sugar
2 tablespoons baking powder
⅓ cup (2½ ounces) grated white chocolate
¼ cup toasted almonds
12 one-half-inch chunks of white chocolate

1. Preheat oven to 325 degrees and grease muffin tins.
2. Combine first 5 ingredients and mix well.
3. Combine remaining ingredients, except the white chocolate chunks, in large bowl and mix well. Make a well in the center and add the wet ingredients. Stir just enough to blend.
4. Fill muffin pans half full. Add one chocolate chunk to each muffin. Add more batter to fill pans three quaters full.
5. Bake in oven about 15 minutes, or until a toothpick inserted into the middle comes out dry.

Wild Blueberry Scones

with Blueberry Sauce

10-12 three-inch scones

Scones—

1½ cups unbleached all-
   purpose flour
½ teaspoon baking soda
1 teaspoon cream of tartar
⅛ teaspoon salt
1 medium egg, lightly beaten
1¼ cups milk
1 tablespoon sugar
½ cup blueberries

Blueberry Sauce—

1 cup fresh blueberries
2 tablespoons lemon juice
1½ cups sugar
Grated peel of one lemon

*Domestic blueberries may be
substituted*

SCONES

1. Sift together flour, baking soda, cream of tartar, and salt.
2. In a separate bowl, mix egg, milk, and sugar. Slowly add this to flour mixture until the batter is thick.
3. Pour ⅓ cup of batter for each scone onto a hot, lightly greased griddle.
4. Drop blueberries onto each scone.
5. When bubbles appear on top of the scone, flip it over.
6. Serve with butter and warm blueberry sauce.

SAUCE

1. Blend blueberries and lemon juice. Fold in sugar and lemon peel.
2. Heat to boiling point stirring continually.
3. Serve with scones.

Onion-Dill Bread

1 loaf

2½ teaspoons active dry yeast
  (¼-ounce package)
2 tablespoons sugar, divided
1¼ cups lukewarm milk
½ cup minced onion
¼ cup fresh minced dill weed or
  2 tablespoons dry dill weed
2 tablespoons softened butter
1 teaspoon salt
1 large egg, lightly beaten
4-5 cups unbleached flour

This should be served warm with lots of butter. It also makes great toast.

1. In a small bowl proof the yeast with 1 teaspoon sugar in ¼ cup milk until it is foamy.
2. In a large bowl combine remaining 1 cup milk and sugar with the onion, dillweed, butter and salt. Stir until butter is melted.
3. Stir in egg and yeast mixture. Add enough flour to make a soft but not sticky dough.
4. Knead the dough on a floured surface for 8-10 minutes until it is smooth and elastic. Form into a ball, transfer to a large oiled bowl, oil the top, cover and let rise until double in bulk.
5. Punch down and let rest 5 minutes. Knead for 1 minute and form into a loaf. Transfer into a greased 9x5x3 inch bread pan and let rise until doubled.
6. Preheat oven to 350 degrees.
7. Bake for 30-45 minutes, or until it sounds hollow when the bottom is tapped. Remove from the pan and cool on a rack.

Old Rittenhouse Inn

Preserves

Wild Blueberry Marmalade

5 to 6 cups

3 cups puréed wild blueberries
½ cup puréed whole orange, seeded
½ cup puréed whole lemon, seeded
1 teaspoon lemon juice
1 package pectin (1¾ ounces)
6 cups sugar

Domestic blueberries may be substituted.

1. In a food processor fitted with a steel blade, separately grind blueberries, orange and lemon.
2. Combine blueberries, orange, lemon, lemon juice, and pectin in a jelly kettle, or large saucepan.
3. Bring to a rolling boil.
4. Add sugar. Bring to a rolling boil, stirring constantly. When mixture boils, stir for 85 seconds.
5. Remove from heat, and let sit 3 minutes.
6. Skim off any film from top of marmalade.
7. Pour into sterilized jars, seal, and process in a water bath according to manufacturer's instructions.

Apple Cider Marmalade

7 cups

**5 cups firm apples, cored and
  slivered (unpeeled)**
1 cup apple cider
½ cup orange juice concentrate
½ cup grated orange rind
½ cup grated lemon rind
1 package pectin (1¾ ounces)
7 cups sugar

*Note: Many varieties of firm
apples will work, but we prefer
Cortlands.*

1. Place apples, cider, orange juice concentrate, rinds and pectin in a large saucepan or jelly kettle. Bring the mixture to a rolling boil.
2. Add sugar and stir until completely dissolved.
3. Bring to a rolling boil again. Boil 65 seconds, stirring constantly.
4. Remove the mixture from the heat. Cool for three minutes.
5. Skim off any foam with a slotted spoon. Ladle into sterilized jars, seal and process in a water bath according to manufacturer's instructions.

Swiss Pear Marmalade

5-6 cups

3 cups puréed pears (cored, stemmed, unpeeled)
½ cup ground whole lemon, seeded
½ cup ground whole orange, seeded
¼ teaspoon ground allspice
⅛ teaspoon ground cinnamon
1 package pectin (1¾ ounces)
6 cups sugar

1. In a food processor fitted with a steel blade, purée the pears and grind the lemon and orange separately.
2. Combine pears, lemon, orange, allspice, and cinnamon in a large, non-aluminum kettle or sauce pan. Add pectin and stir well. Bring to a boil.
3. Add sugar. Stirring continually, bring mixture to a rolling boil.
4. While boiling, stir for 85 seconds. Remove from heat. Remove spoon from mixture. Let stand for 3 minutes. Carefully skim foam off top.
5. Pour in sterilized jars, seal and process in a water bath according to manufacturer's instructions.

Red Raspberry Jam

5 cups

5 cups puréed red raspberries
1 tablespoon lemon juice
1 package pectin (1¾ ounce)
6 cups sugar

1. Bring raspberries, lemon juice, and pectin to a rolling boil in a large, non-aluminum kettle.
2. Add sugar, stirring well.
3. Bring to a rolling boil. Boil for 85 seconds, stirring continually. Remove from heat. Cool 3 minutes. Remove skim from top.
4. Pour into sterilized jars, seal and process in a water bath according to manufacturer's instructions.

Crab Apple Jelly

6 cups

3 pounds fresh whole crab
  apples
6 cups cold water
1 package pectin (1¾ ounces)
6 cups sugar

1. Remove stems from crab apples. Place them in a large kettle and add the water. Bring to a rolling boil, reduce heat, and cook until the apples split (about 15 minutes).
2. Line a colander with a double layer of cheesecloth and place it over a large mixing bowl. Pour the contents of the kettle into colander and let juices drip for several hours. This should yield 4 cups of juice.
3. Clean the kettle and return the juice to it. Add pectin and heat until juice begins to boil. Add sugar and stir in well.
4. Bring to boil and stir for 75 seconds.
5. Remove from heat and let set for several minutes. Skim off foam. Immediately pour into sterilized jars, seal and process in a water bath according to manufacturer's directions.

Peach Chardonnay Jelly

6 cups

3½ cups peach juice*
¼ cup grapefruit juice
¼ chardonnay wine
⅛ teaspoon freshly grated
     ginger
1 package pectin (1¾ ounces)
3 cups sugar

Use juice from canned peaches in light syrup. If you use fresh peaches, you will need more sugar.

1. Combine juices, chardonnay, ginger, and pectin in large jelly kettle, and bring to a rolling boil.
2. Add sugar and stir in well. Bring to a rolling boil, stirring constantly. When mixture is boiling, stir for 85 seconds. Remove from heat.
3. Let stand for three minutes. Skim any foam from top of jelly.
4. Pour into sterilized jars, seal and process in a water bath according to manufacturer's instructions.

Old Rittenhouse Inn

Accompaniments

Cranberry Sorbet

2 quarts

3 twelve-ounce cans frozen
   cranberry juice concentrate
1 twelve-ounce can frozen
   cranberry/apple juice
   concentrate
1 twelve-ounce can frozen
   lemonade concentrate
1 twenty-four-ounce bottle
   sparkling white grape juice
   (non-alcoholic)
1 tablespoon peeled, finely
   grated fresh ginger root

Garnish—

Fresh mint
Sliced fresh cranberries

1. Combine all ingredients.
2. Freeze according to ice cream machine
   manufacturer's instructions.
3. Garnish with sprig of fresh mint and
   cranberries.

Gingered Lemon Sorbet

2 quarts

3 cups lemon juice, freshly
   squeezed
3 cups orange juice, freshly
   squeezed
3 cups water
4 cups sugar
½ cup freshly grated ginger root
1 cup unsweetened white grape
   juice

Garnish—

Blueberries
Fresh mint

1. Combine all ingredients.
2. Freeze according to ice cream machine manufacturer's instructions.
3. Garnish with blueberries and a sprig of fresh mint.

Cranberry Orange Relish

5-6 cups

1 whole orange, seeded and
  quartered
2 cups cranberries
1 cup english walnut pieces,
  coarsely chopped
4 cups finely slivered apples,
  with peel
¾ cup honey
1 tablespoon fresh grated ginger

1. Run orange quarters through food processor fitted with a steel blade until finely chopped. Add cranberries and process for 3-5 seconds, or until coarsely chopped. Remove from processor and place in a medium size mixing bowl.
2. Fold in walnuts, apples, honey and ginger.
3. Cover, and refrigerate 3 hours before serving.

Papaya Relish

4 cups

2 ripe papayas, seeded (about 1
pound each)
1 cup chopped pineapple,
peeled and cored
1 jalapeno pepper, red or green,
finely minced
1 large clove garlic, peeled and
minced
½ cup finely chopped purple
onion
¼ cup chopped cilantro
½ cup fresh lime juice

1. Peel papayas and chop into ¼ inch pieces.
   Place in a medium sized bowl and toss with
   pineapple.
2. Add remaining ingredients and combine
   well. Chill at least 4 hours before serving.

Cranberry Chutney

6 cups

5 cups cranberry-orange relish
(see recipe on page 90)
1 cup cranberry juice
1 package pectin (1¾ ounces)
5 cups sugar

1. Heat relish, cranberry juice and pectin in a jelly kettle or large sauce pan and bring to a boil.
2. Add sugar. Stirring slowly, bring to a rolling boil. Allow to boil 85 seconds while stirring.
3. Remove from heat. Let stand 3 minutes. Skim any foam.
4. Pour into sterilized jars, seal and process in a water bath according to manufacturer's instructions.

Green Onion Relish

3 cups

1 cup diced, whole green onions
2 cups seeded puréed tomatoes
   with skins on
1 cup chopped celery
½ cup chopped green bell
   pepper
½ cup chopped yellow bell
   pepper
1 teaspoon ground cumin
1 teaspoon paprika
1 large clove garlic, peeled and
   puréed

1. Combine all ingredients.
2. Refrigerate for 24 hours in a covered container.
3. Stir the mixture and serve.

Smoked Trout Butter

1 cup

¼ pound unsalted butter
2 teaspoons chopped dill
4 ounces smoked trout, flaked
1 teaspoon lemon juice

1. Soften butter.
2. Process butter, dill, trout and lemon juice in a food processor.
3. Form mixture into desired shape and chill.

Herbed Butter

2½ cups

**1 pound butter softened at
   room temperature**
½ cup puréed fresh spinach
1 tablespoon chopped parsley
1 tablespoon chopped chives
2 tablespoons lemon juice
Salt and pepper to taste

1. Combine butter, spinach, parsley, chives, lemon juice, salt and pepper.
2. Process 5 seconds in food processor, using steel blade.
3. Ladle into individual butter molds and chill, or chill and form as desired.

Rittenhouse Reddening

1 part curry, ground
1 part white pepper
1 part red cayenne pepper
1 part sesame seeds
2 parts onion powder
3 parts garlic powder
6 parts paprika

1. Blend all ingredients until evenly mixed throughout.
2. Store in a tightly covered container in a dry place.

Apple-Rhubarb Chutney

1½ quarts

2 cups chopped rhubarb
2 cups chopped apples
2 teaspoons minced garlic
1 cup golden raisins
1 cup dark raisins
1 cup light brown sugar
½ cup honey
⅓ cup ground lemon rind
⅓ cup ground orange rind
2 tablespoons orange juice
    concentrate
¼ cup lemonade concentrate
⅓ cup cranberry concentrate
1 tablespoon fresh grated ginger
    root
¾ teaspoon ground cinnamon
⅛ teaspoon ground cloves
⅛ teaspoon ground cumin

May be served warm or cold as a condiment, or may be water packed in a jar for later use.

1. Combine all ingredients in a large saucepan and bring to a boil, stirring frequently. Lower heat and cook until mixture is thick.

Old Rittenhouse Inn

Sauces

Raisin Sauce

3 cups

1 cup brown sugar
1 tablespoon flour
1 tablespoon cornstarch
¼ teaspoon curry
4 tablespoons orange juice
    concentrate
4 tablespoons lemon juice
½ teaspoon grated lemon rind
2½ cups orange juice
½ cup brandy
1½ cups golden raisins

1. Thoroughly mix brown sugar, flour, corn-starch, and curry in a medium size bowl.
2. In another bowl, combine orange juice concentrate, lemon rind, and orange juice. Add to the sugar mixture and transfer to a saucepan.
3. Cook over low heat, stirring slowly until sauce begins to thicken. Add brandy and raisins. Continue to cook until raisins puff. Remove from heat.

Juniper Berry Sauce

2½ cups

2 tablespoons butter
3 tablespoons white flour or rice
  flour
1 cup beef stock
1 cup water
½ cup dry red wine
1 tablespoon ground juniper
  berries

This is an excellent sauce to serve with duck, goose, or wild game.

1. Melt butter in a medium sized sauce pan. Add flour and blend until smooth.
2. Add beef stock, water and red wine. Stir over medium heat until thickened.
3. Stir in juniper berries. Cook for 1 minute over low heat. Remove from heat.

Cranberry Salsa

3¼ cups

2 cups chopped cranberries
1 cup chopped tomatoes,
  unpeeled and seeded
¼ cup hot salsa
1 tablespoon lemon juice

1. Combine all ingredients in a blender or food processor fitted with a steel blade.
2. Cover and chill overnight.

Tomato-Basil Sauce

1½ cups

1 tablespoon olive oil
½ cup onions, chopped
2 cups seeded and chopped ripe
  tomatoes
4 large garlic cloves
2 tablespooons chopped fresh
  basil
Salt and pepper to taste

1. Heat olive oil in heavy, non-aluminum sauté pan. Add onions and sauté until opaque.
2. Add tomatoes, garlic, basil, salt, pepper.
3. Cook over low heat 20 minutes.
4. Remove from heat. Purée in food processor fitted with a steel blade.

Whipped Horseradish Cream

2 cups

½ cup prepared creamed horseradish
¼ cup finely chopped onion
2 teaspoons lemon juice
1 teaspoon anchovy paste
¼ teaspoon rubbed sage
½ teaspoon ground cumin
¼ teaspoon ground black pepper
1½ cup whipped heavy cream

This is good served with beef or pork.

1. Combine horseradish, onion, lemon juice, anchovy paste and seasonings in a medium size bowl.
2. Gently fold in whipped cream.
3. Chill well before serving.

Blender Bearnaise

1½ cups

3 egg yolks at room
   temperature
¼ pound melted butter (hot)
½ cup dry white wine
1 tablespoon lemon juice
1 tablespoon chopped onion
2 teaspoons finely chopped
   tarragon
¼ teaspoon white pepper
Salt and cayenne to taste

1. In a blender or food processor fitted with a steel blade, blend egg yolks. Slowly add hot butter while blending. Blend until thick.
2. Add wine, then lemon, onion, tarragon, pepper, salt, and cayenne. Blend to combine.
3. Keep warm to serve.

Blender Hollandaise

1½ cups

1 cup melted butter (140
    degrees)
4 egg yolks
1 tablespoon lemon juice
¼ teaspoon Tabasco sauce
1 teaspoon chicken base

*Note: Egg yolks and lemon
should be at room temperature.*

1. Use thermometer to make sure butter is at 140 degrees.
2. In a food processor fitted with a steel blade, or in a blender, process egg yolks, lemon juice, Tabasco sauce, and chicken base.
3. With processor covered and running, slowly add hot butter in a steady stream. Blend until thick and creamy.

Garlic Mayonnaise

1¼ cups

1 cup mayonnaise
2 tablespoons heavy whipping
  cream
2-3 garlic cloves, peeled and
  minced
1 teaspoon fresh basil
1 teaspoon fresh tarragon
1 teaspoon lemon juice

1. Combine all ingredients in a food processor, fitted with a steel blade or in a blender.
2. Blend until smooth.
3. Cover and refrigerate until used.

Tartar Sauce

1½ cups

1½ cups mayonnaise
2 tablespoons fresh lemon juice
⅛ cup sweet pickle relish
⅛ cup chopped onion
½ tablespoon creamed
   horseradish
3 drops Tabasco sauce
Dash of curry powder
½ tablespoon capers (optional)

1. In a small bowl, mix all ingredients. Chill before serving.

Garlic & Sage Sauce with Pinenuts

1½ cups

8-10 cloves minced fresh garlic
1 tablespoon minced fresh sage
1 cup olive oil
2 egg yolks, warmed
1 tablespoon fresh lemon juice
¼ cup pinenuts, roasted
salt and pepper to taste

This sauce is great with lake trout.

1. Combine garlic, sage and olive oil in blender or food processor fitted with steel blade. Blend until thick and smooth.
2. Add yolks and lemon juice and blend.
3. Place in glass or stainless steel bowl and add pinenuts. Salt and pepper to taste. Refrigerate for several hours to blend the flavors. Serve at room temperature.

Old Rittenhouse Inn

Meats

Steak Bercy

6 servings

Sauce—

¾ cup melted butter
2 tablespoons chopped green onions
½ cup dry red wine
2 tablespoons chopped parsley
1 tablespoon lemon juice
½ tablespoon beef base
3 cloves minced garlic
12 large mushroom caps

Entree—

6 eight-ounce filet mignons
Salt and pepper to taste

Garnish—

Mushroom caps

SAUCE
1. Combine all ingredients including the mushroom caps, and simmer for 15 minutes.

ENTREE
1. Grill steaks to desired liking, brushing several times with the sauce. Season to taste with salt and pepper.
2. Pour 1 tablespoon sauce over each steak and serve immediately.
3. Garnish with mushroom caps.

Carpet-Bagger Bercy

Follow recipe for Steak Bercy, except prior to grilling, split steak to make a pocket, and fill steak with 4 ounces sautéed oysters.

Beef Stroganoff

8 servings

**3 pounds top sirloin, cubed or
cut in thin strips**
8 tablespoons butter or olive oil
**2 large sweet onions, thinly
sliced (about 3 cups)**
½ cup sour cream
2 tablespoons tomato paste
1 cup slivered mushrooms
Salt and fresh grated pepper

*Note: This is a very simple dish,
requiring quickness of preparation
and the freshest and best of
ingredients. If you can, use wild
mushrooms like morels. You may
also add ¼ cup sherry or cognac.*

1. Sauté beef one minute in butter or oil on medium high heat in a large skillet, turning frequently.
2. Reduce heat to medium, add onion, and sauté one minute, stirring continually.
3. Remove from heat, transfer beef to warm bowl and keep warm.
4. Stirring continually, combine sour cream and tomato paste in skillet until smooth.
5. Return skillet to low heat, adding mushrooms and beef. Season to taste with salt and pepper and heat to warm.
6. Serve over rice or noodles; or if you wish to be more authentic, over kasha, roasted buckwheat groats.

Beef Benedict

6 servings

6 six ounce fillet mignons
6 slices ham or Canadian bacon,
   cut to fit steak
6 poached eggs
hollandaise sauce (about ¼ cup
   per serving)

Garnish—

Paprika
12 spears asparagus, cooked
   just until tender

1. Grill fillets to desired doneness.
2. While grilling, poach eggs.
3. Assemble by placing steak on heated plate. Place ham on top of steak, eggs on top of ham, and ladle hollandaise over all.

Garnish with paprika and serve with asparagus spears on the side.

Apple Glazed Pork Chops

6 servings

6 pork chops, center cut
  (about 2 inches thick and
  1 pound in weight, each)
4 tablespoons vegetable oil
4 cups reduced beef broth
½ cup dry red wine
1 teaspoon minced thyme
1 teaspoon minced marjoram
1 teaspoon minced basil
1 teaspoon minced summer
  savory
1 tablespoon minced fresh garlic
4 tablespoons flour
5 tablespoons cold water
Apple Cider Marmalade (see
  recipe on page 81)

To produce a rich broth which adds greatly to the flavor of this entree, simply cook regular beef stock down to half—then use this reduced stock for recipe. Adding ½ cup of red wine also adds flavor.

1. Preheat oven to 325 degrees.
2. In a heavy preheated skillet, brown the chops in oil over medium heat, 10 minutes on each side or until well browned.
3. Arrange chops in roasting pan. Pour beef broth and wine over chops. Add thyme, marjoram, basil, savory and garlic.
4. Cover and bake at 325 degrees for 2 to 3 hours, or until fork tender.
5. When pork chops are done, remove chops from oven and keep warm.
6. Strain pan juices and skim off fat. Measure 3 cups of pan juices and transfer to a saucepan.
7. Blend flour and water in small bowl until smooth. Whisk into pan juices. Cook over medium heat until thickened. Reduce heat to low and simmer 3 minutes, stirring occasionally.
8. Ladle brown sauce onto a warm plate. Arrange a pork chop in the center of each plate. Spoon warm apple marmalade over each chop.

Pictured on page 13 of Old Rittenhouse History.

Pork Chops in Cream

6 servings

Entree—

½ teaspoon ground white pepper
2 tablespoon minced fresh garlic
1 tablespoon minced fresh thyme
1 tablespoon minced fresh basil
½ teaspoon caraway seed
4 tablespoons olive or vegetable oil
6 two-inch thick center-cut pork chops
1½ cups beef stock
1 tablespoon butter
1 tablespoon flour
3 tablespoons Cognac
4 tablespoons chopped scallions
3 cups finely chopped fresh mushrooms
1 cup light cream
3 large egg yolks
Salt and white pepper to taste

Garnish—

Fresh minced parsley
Fresh minced chives

1. Preheat oven to 325 degrees.
2. Mix first 5 ingredients in a small bowl. Sprinkle pork chops with the seasoning and press into both sides.
3. Heat oil on medium high heat in a large skillet until it sizzles. Add the chops and sear until brown. Turn over and sear on other side.
4. Arrange chops in a single layer in the bottom of a roasting pan reserving juice in skillet. Pour beef stock over chops, cover pan, and bake in preheated oven until fork tender—at least 1½ hours.
5. Save the beef stock in a tightly covered container in the freezer and use for soup or for making pork chops another time.
6. Melt butter in a skillet over medium heat. Add flour and whisk until smooth. Fold in Cognac; set aside.
7. Reheat the skillet that was used to brown the chops. Add scallions and mushrooms. Heat through.
8. Add ½ cup cream. Cook slowly over medium heat until mushrooms yield some juice. Bring just to a boil.
9. Slowly whisk in the flour-Cognac mixture until sauce is well combined and slightly thickened.
10. Combine egg yolks and remaining cream in a small bowl. Whisk well to blend.
11. Add a small amount of the hot sauce to the yolks and cream, then slowly pour mixture into the skillet containing the scallions and mushrooms, whisking steadily to avoid curdling the egg yolks. Taste and adjust seasonings. Place a pork chop on each of six heated serving plates. Spoon sauce over and around chops. Garnish with parsley and chives.

Lamb Ragoût

6 servings

3 pounds boneless lamb
   shoulder, cut in 1½ inch
   pieces.
2 tablespoons butter
1 tablespoon vegetable oil
2 teaspoons paprika
2 teaspoons sugar
4 cups lamb or beef stock
½ cup dry red wine
¼ teaspoon ground pepper
4 minced garlic cloves
1 teaspoon minced fresh
   rosemary
1 teaspoon fresh minced thyme
1 bay leaf
6 new red potatoes
2 large carrots, cut crosswise
   into 2-inch pieces
1 cup green string beans
1 large onion, cut into 6 pieces
3 medium tomatoes, cut into 4
   pieces each
6 large mushroom caps
4 tablespoons flour
5 tablespoons cold water
6 one-half cup servings of
   cooked, buttered and parslied
   noodles

Garnish—

Sour cream
Mint leaves

1. Preheat oven to 325 degrees.
2. Heat butter and oil on medium heat in a large skillet. Brown lamb pieces and transfer to a 4-quart casserole.
3. Add paprika and sugar to butter, oil, and lamb drippings. Cook until the sugar melts. Remove from heat. Reserve.
4. Add stock and wine to the lamb, along with pepper, garlic, rosemary, thyme, and bay leaf.
5. Cover and place in a 325-degree oven.
6. Bake for 20 minutes. Add potatoes and carrots. Return to oven and bake 10 minutes. Add beans, onion, tomato and mushrooms. Bake for 10-15 minutes until lamb is done and vegetables are tender.
7. Remove casserole from oven and transfer liquid to skillet from step #3. Adjust seasoning to taste.
8. In a small bowl combine flour and cold water into a smooth paste. Add to juices, and cook on medium heat until thickened.
9. Add lamb and vegetables.
10. Serve ragoût over parslied buttered noodles. Top with sour cream and a sprig of fresh mint.

Veal Paprikash

6 servings

3 pounds boneless veal
    shoulder, cut in 1½ inch
    pieces
2 tablespoons butter
2 tablespoons oil
1 cup onions, chopped
½ cup green bell peppers,
    seeded and chopped
½ cup red bell pepper, seeded
    and chopped
3 garlic cloves, minced
2 tablespoons hungarian
    paprika
⅛ teaspoon cayenne pepper,
    ground
White pepper, thyme, tarragon
    to taste
2 cups veal stock (or beef)
1 cup blended fresh tomatoes,
    seeded
¼-½ cup sour cream
3-4 cups noodles, cooked,
    tossed with butter and poppy
    seeds

Garnishes—

Sour cream sauce
Pimentos
Finely chopped fresh parsley

1. Preheat oven to 325 degrees.
2. In a large skillet or sauté pan, heat the butter and oil. Brown veal on all sides. Transfer veal to a 4 quart casserole dish.
3. In the same pan sauté onions, peppers, and garlic until onions are soft and transparent. Add seasonings, stock, and tomatoes. Pour on top of the veal.
4. Cook covered at 325 degrees for 30 minutes, or until veal is fork tender. If necessary add more stock.
5. Remove from oven , uncover casserole, and skim off fat. Check and correct seasoning to taste.
6. Pour 1 cup of casserole liquid into a saucepan. Fold in sour cream, and cook over very low heat, stirring until mixture reaches desired thickness. Remove from heat.
7. Serve veal over buttered poppy seed noodles. Top with sour cream sauce from step #6. Sprinkle pimentos and chopped parsley on top.

Roast Leg of Lamb

8 servings

5-6 pound leg of lamb
3-4 quarts stock, or make this
  stock;
    3-4 quarts water
    ¼ cup beef base
    ¼ cup chicken base
1 cup merlot or red zinfindel
  wine
¼ cup minced fresh garlic
2 tablespoons minced fresh
  rosemary
2 tablespoons minced fresh
  thyme
1 tablespoon minced fresh sage
1 teaspoon cracked pepper
3 bay leaves
¼ cup fresh lemon juice
4 tablespoons rice flour
½ cup cold water

1. Preheat oven to 350 degrees.
2. Place lamb in a deep-sided baking pan and add enough stock to cover half the lamb.
3. Score lamb with a sharp knife in a criss-cross pattern. Pour wine over lamb and sprinkle garlic, rosemary, thyme, basil, sage and pepper over lamb and liquid. Add bay leaves to liquid and cover tightly.
4. Bake to desired doneness (45-60 minutes for medium rare to medium).
5. Remove from oven and strain juices into a very large skillet. Place skillet on high heat and reduce to 4-5 cups of liquid.
6. Meanwhile, pierce the lamb throughout with a sharp fork or knife and drizzle with fresh lemon juice. Cover lamb and keep warm until stock is reduced.
7. When stock is reduced to 4-5 cups, make into a sauce by adding rice flour mixed into ½ cup cold water. Stir continuously while adding and bring to boil. Reduce heat and keep warm until served.

Old Rittenhouse Inn

Poultry

Brandied Chicken Breasts

with Bayfield Cherries

8 servings

½ pound melted butter or
   margarine
⅔ cup brandy
⅔ cup sherry
2 tablespoons cherry jelly
2 tablespoons Worcestershire
   sauce
¼ teaspoon red cayenne
   pepper—ground
¼ teaspoon allspice—ground
¼ teaspoon cumin—ground
½ teaspoon curry powder
½ tablespoon grated ginger root
1 tablesoon minced fresh garlic
1 teaspoon paprika
1 teaspoon salt
1 teaspoon pepper
8 chicken breasts, boned and
   skinned
4 teaspoons cornstarch
4 tablespoons water
2 cups pitted red sweet cherries
6 cups cooked wild rice

1. Combine first 14 ingredients in a large skillet. Simmer and stir until jelly is dissolved.
2. Add chicken breasts. Simmer until cooked through, turning breasts occassionally. Remove breasts from skillet, and keep warm.
3. Blend cornstarch and water until smooth. Add to the liquid in skillet. Stir over low heat until sauce is thickened.
4. Fold in cherries and heat through.
5. Place hot cooked wild rice on serving plates, and top with chicken breasts.
6. Spoon cherry sauce over breasts and serve.

Rittenhouse Cordon Bleu

8 servings

8 ounces cream cheese
1 ounce sour cream
4 ounces shredded cheddar
   cheese
2 ounces shredded swiss
   cheese
2 ounces grated parmesan
   cheese
1 ounce crumbled feta cheese
8 slices cooked ham, thinly
   sliced
8 chicken breasts, skinned and
   boned
2-3 cups chicken stock
1 tablespoon fresh basil,
   chopped
1 tablespoon fresh thyme,
   chopped

Garnish—

2 cups hollandaise sauce (see
   recipe on page 106)
½ cup slivered almonds

1. Preheat oven to 350 degrees.
2. Combine first 6 ingredients until evenly mixed.
3. Stuff each breast with a slice of ham and ⅛ of the cheese mixture. Roll up the chicken breasts and place seam down in a baking pan.
4. Pour chicken stock over the breasts. Sprinkle with basil and thyme. Bake uncovered at 350 degrees for one hour, or until done.
5. Remove from pan. Top each breast with hollandaise and slivered almonds.

Cilantro Chicken

8 servings

8 skinned and boneless chicken breasts
1 cup lime juice
1 cup lemon juice
1 ½ cups dry white wine
½ cup olive oil
1 ½ cups chopped cilantro
4 cloves minced garlic
1 tablespoon fresh chopped rosemary
1 tablespoon fresh chopped tarragon
1 tablespoon coarsely ground pepper
2 teaspoons coarse sea salt

Garnish—

3 avocados, peeled
2 vine ripened tomatoes, sliced
Fresh cilantro leaves

Papaya relish is a fine accompaniment. (See recipe on page 91)

1. Place chicken breasts in a large, shallow roasting pan. Combine the remaining ingredients and pour over the chicken.
2. Cover and marinate 1 hour, stirring several times to season.
3. Preheat oven to 350 degrees.
4. Remove chicken from marinade. Place in casserole or baking dish with ½ cup of the marinade and bake covered for 15 minutes.
5. Uncover and bake until tender and lightly browned.
6. Garnish with avocado, tomato slices, and cilantro.

Escalloped Chicken

6-8 servings

5 tablespoons butter
6 tablespoons flour
1 cup half and half
1 cup chicken stock
¼ teaspoon paprika
½ teaspoon minced garlic
¼ teaspoon curry
3 cups chicken (ground in processor with a steel blade)
¼ cup chopped green bell peppers
⅛ cup chopped red bell peppers
1 cup sliced mushrooms
¼ cup chopped onions
½ cup cheese, shredded
1 cup buttered bread crumbs

1. Preheat oven to 300 degrees and grease a one-quart baking dish.
2. Melt butter in medium sauce pan. Add flour and mix until smooth.
3. Mix cream and chicken stock, and add to flour/butter. Cook over medium heat, stirring continually until thick and creamy. Remove from heat.
4. Add seasonings, chicken, peppers, mushrooms, and onions.
5. Pour into a baking dish. Sprinkle with shredded cheese. Cover with bread crumbs. Bake at 300 degrees for 30 minutes.

Terrine of Chicken

8 servings

Terrine—

2 pounds cooked, skinned, diced chicken
½ pound fresh spinach leaves, chopped (4 cups)
¾ cup heavy cream
½ cup dry white wine
5 eggs
2 teaspoons salt
1 teaspoon white pepper
2 teaspoons ground rosemary or tarragon
2 tablespoons lemon juice
4 cloves garlic minced
½ cup onion, minced
Fresh leaves (spinach or grape)

Sauce—

5 tablespoons sour cream
1 tablespoon cognac
3 drops tabasco sauce

Garnish—

Fresh cilantro leaves

Although this terrine is to be chilled, it can also be served warm with good results.

TERRINE

1. Preheat oven to 350 degrees.
2. Pureé chicken in food processor. Add spinach, cream, wine, eggs, seasonings, lemon juice, garlic, and onion. Process until smooth. Place in greased mold, lined with fresh leaves (spinach, grape, or other).
3. Cover with more leaves. Place terrine in a shallow pan of water and put in the center of the oven. Bake until set (30-35 minutes).
4. Remove from oven and chill well. Unmold, garnish and serve with sauce.

SAUCE

1. Blend all the sauce ingredients.
2. Serve with sauce drizzled over the top of each slice of terrine and garnish with cilantro leaves.

Poulet a la Champagne

4 servings

4 whole chicken breasts, boned, skinned and halved
4 tablespoons butter
1 teaspoon Rittenhouse Reddening (see recipe on page 96)
1 cup champagne
3 tablespoons orange liqueur
1 cup chicken stock
½ cup sour cream or heavy whipping cream
2 tablespoons butter
1 cup shiitake mushrooms
¼ cup minced fresh chives

1. Preheat oven to 325 degrees.
2. Sauté chicken breasts in butter for 4 to 5 minutes.
3. Remove chicken to baking dish and bake covered for 15 minutes. Reserve juices in sauté pan.
4. Add champagne, liqueur, chicken stock and 4 tablespoons butter to reserved juices in sauté pan. Bring to a simmer.
5. Add sour cream or heavy cream to the champagne mixture and simmer until thick.
6. In another pan melt 2 tablespoons butter. Add mushrooms and sauté. Mix in chives. Keep warm.
7. Place chicken and sautéed mushrooms on pasta or rice. Spoon champagne sauce over the top.

Old Rittenhouse Inn

Seafood

En croûte de la Mer

4 servings

¾-1 pound lake trout (or
 salmon) fillets
¾-1 pound Lake Superior
 whitefish fillets
½ pound smoked whitefish,
 boned and flaked
¼ pound butter
½ teaspoon dill weed
White pepper to taste
Filo dough
Fresh spinach
Alfalfa sprouts

Garnish—

Scallops
¼ pound butter
Curry to taste (⅛ teaspoon)

_If you wish, the encroute can be
served with a sauce; although we
prefer a simple herbed drawn
butter and lemon wedges. We
often garnish this with three or
four scallops for each serving,
which we sauté for five minutes
in butter with a touch of curry._

_Pictured on page 12 of
Old Rittenhouse History._

1. Place trout fillet, skin down, on shallow buttered baking sheet and bake in preheated 350-degree oven until just underdone (10 minutes). Remove from oven to refrigerator and chill 1 hour minimum.
2. Place whitefish fillet, skin down, in sauté pan in which ¼ pound of butter has been melted. Sprinkle with dill weed and white pepper and sauté on medium heat until just under done. To remove, slide a long turner between skin and flesh, and transfer to refrigerator with trout. While fish are chilling, thaw filo dough.
3. When the fish are chilled, unroll filo dough. (Dough should measure approximately 11 by 15 inches.) Cover with a cloth as you assemble remaining ingredients. Center 5 to 7 leaves of filo dough on a lightly buttered baking sheet. Place chilled trout in center, lengthwise, stretching 11 or 12 inches. This may require 2 fillets. Cover this with a double thickness of fresh spinach leaves. On top of this add a layer of the smoked whitefish. Now add a layer of sprouts and then the fillet of chilled whitefish. Finish with another layer of spinach. Draw up ends of the filo dough over the layers and seal edges with a light brushing of water. Brush the En croute with melted butter, sprinkle with paprika, and it is ready to bake or refrigerate for later use.
4. Bake in preheated oven at 350 degrees for 15-20 minutes, until golden brown on top. Serve immediately, slicing like French bread, therefore exposing the layers.

This dish is especially attractive, with layers of fish and greens alternating top to bottom. But is also very convenient because it can be assembled ahead of time and chilled. Then, 15-20 minutes before serving time put into oven and finish.

Reddened Trout

8 servings

Entree—

8 ounces bread crumbs
½ cup dry dill, chopped
3 tablespoons garlic powder
1 tablespoon salt
½ cup Old Rittenhouse Inn
   Reddening (see recipe on
   page 96)
4 pounds fresh trout fillets
½ cup melted butter

Sauce—

½ pound softened butter
1 tablespoon fresh minced garlic
2 tablespoons Reddening
½ cup tomato paste
½ teaspoon tabasco sauce

ENTREE

1. Process bread crumbs, dill, garlic powder, salt and Rittenhouse Reddening in a food processor with a steel blade.
2. Cover flesh side of fillet with crumb mixture.
3. Place fillet in large skillet, skin down, with melted butter. Cover and cook until fish flakes.
4. Remove fish from sauté pan. Put them on plates, with sauce on the side.

SAUCE

1. In a food processor fitted with a steel blade, process softened butter, fresh garlic, Rittenhouse Reddening, tomato paste, and tabasco sauce.

Lake Superior Trout Meuniere

8 servings

8 small fresh trout (about 4
   pounds)
2 cups milk
½ to ¾ cup flour
1 teaspoon salt
½ teaspoon black pepper,
   coarsely ground
2 teaspoons fresh minced herbs
   (dill, fennel, chervil, tarragon,
   thyme, or combinations of
   these)
¼-½ pound butter, melted

Garnish—

4 tablespoons butter, melted
Lemon slices
Fresh parsley

1. Clean fish and rinse well under cold running water.
2. Place the fish in a shallow pan. Cover with milk and let stand for 30 to 45 minutes at room temperature.
3. Remove from milk and drain, but do not dry.
4. Mix flour, salt, pepper and herbs. Coat fish one at a time in seasoned flour. Use additional flour as needed.
5. Put enough melted butter in a large skillet to fill ⅛ inch deep.
6. Add trout, skin down, and cook on medium heat until golden brown. Turn and cook other side.
7. Remove skin and transfer fish to serving platter.
8. Garnish with thin slices of lemon and fresh parsley sprigs and drizzle with butter.

Smoked Trout

with Black Olive Fettucini

6-8 servings

1 pound fettuccini, uncooked
2-3 garlic cloves, peeled and
   minced (or ¼ cup chopped
   wild leeks)
½ cup slivered green stuffed
   olives
½ cup slivered black olives
½ cup fresh chanterelle or
   shiitake mushroom caps.
8 ounces flaked smoked trout
2 tablespoons of melted butter
   or olive oil
4 tablespoons olive oil or melted
   butter
1 tablespoon lemon juice
Cracked pepper to taste
5 ounces fresh grated parmesan
   cheese
1 egg yolk at room temperature
½ cup heavy, (whipping) cream,
   warm

*Smoked Whitefish, Sole, Herring,
or Salmon may be substituted.*

1. Cook fettucini al dente (still firm to bite) in a large kettle of water, kept to a rolling boil.
2. While pasta is cooking, combine garlic, olives, mushrooms, smoked trout and melted butter in sauté pan and sauté 5 minutes, stirring. Keep warm.
3. When fettuccini is cooked but still firm, transfer to colander and drain well.
4. In a large bowl, toss pasta with oil or butter, lemon and cracked pepper.
5. Add cheese, egg yolk and heavy cream. Toss.
6. Serve fettuccini topped with smoked trout mixture from step #2.

Grilled Whitefish

with Red Pepper Butter

6-8 servings

Whitefish—

4 pounds whitefish fillets
4 tablespoons vegetable oil
4 tablespoons olive oil
2 tablespoons lime juice
1 teaspoon fresh fennel, chopped
1 teaspoon fresh basil, minced
½ teaspoon fresh cilantro, chopped
Salt and pepper to taste

Red Pepper Butter—

1 pound softened butter
½ pound chopped red peppers
3 tablespoons dark mustard
2 large garlic cloves, peeled and minced
1 teaspoon Worcestershire sauce
1 teaspoon soy sauce
1 teaspoon freshly ground ginger

Garnish—

Lime and lemon slices

WHITEFISH

1. Brush hot grill with vegetable oil to avoid sticking.
2. Place fillets, skin down on grill.
3. Brush fish with mixture of olive oil and lime juice.
4. Sprinkle fillets with fresh fennel, basil and cilentro.
5. Salt and pepper to taste
6. Grill for 5 minutes. Turn, remove skin, and grill to your degree of doneness.
7. Serve with red pepper butter and garnish.

RED PEPPER BUTTER

1. Combine all ingredients and process, using steel blade, until smooth and creamy.
2. Form into individual shapes or ramekins and chill until firm.

Whitefish Livers

with Chanterelles

2 servings

Entree—

1 pound whitefish livers (trout or
   cod livers may be substituted)
8 fresh basil leaves, chopped
3 tablespoons flour
¼ cup butter
4 tablespoons dry white dry wine
1 cup chanterelle mushrooms
½ cup fresh whipping cream
Salt and cracked pepper

Garnish—

4 slices crisped bacon,
   crumbled
½ cup chives or green onion
   tops, chopped

On the side—

Horseradish or horseradish
   sauce

*Shiitake mushrooms are also
great with Whitefish livers.*

*A horseradish sauce makes a
great accompaniment.*

ENTREE

1. Rinse the livers in cold water, drain, blot dry on a paper towel.
2. Put them on a flat pan, sprinkle basil and flour over them, and toss until coated.
3. Heat butter in a skillet. Add livers and sauté until browned on all sides (1 or 2 minutes). Add white wine, chanterelles. Simmer for 3 minutes. Add cream slowly, stirring. Salt and pepper to taste.
4. Serve over noodles, toast, or wild rice.
5. Garnish with bacon and chives.

Shrimp and Scallops

in Gingered Peanut Sauce

6 servings

Entree—

- 4 tablespoons olive oil
- 1 pound raw headless shrimp, peeled and deveined
- 1 pound scallops
- Curry to taste
- ½ cup finely chopped onions
- 2 medium tomatoes, coarsely chopped
- 1 Jalapeno pepper, seeded and finely chopped
- 3 cups cooked rice

Sauce—

- ¼ cup peanuts
- ½ cup grated coconut
- 1 cup milk
- 1 tablespoon coriander
- 1 tablespoon grated fresh ginger
- ⅛ tablespoon white pepper
- 1 tablespoon white flour
- ⅛ teaspoon Chinese hot oil, or to taste
- 2 tablespoons lime juice

ENTREE
1. In a heavy skillet, heat the oil. Cook the shrimp and scallops for 2-3 minutes, seasoning with curry, turning them frequently. The shrimp should be firm and pink. The scallops should be opaque. Remove shrimp and scallops and keep warm.
2. Saute onions in the same oil until soft and transparent. Add tomatoes and pepper. Reduce heat to low and simmer for 5 minutes. Remove from heat and add seafood. Keep warm until served.

SAUCE
Combine all sauce ingredients in a food processor fitted with a steel blade. Process until creamy and smooth.

ASSEMBLY
Serve shrimp and scallop mixture over hot rice. Pour peanut sauce over top or serve on side.

Shrimp with Salsa

6 servings

36 large green headless raw shrimp, shelled and deveined
¼ pound melted butter
½ cup chopped onion
1 cup chopped green bell pepper
½ cup chopped red bell pepper
1 cup tomatoes, cored, seeded and chopped
4 cloves garlic, minced
¼ cup chopped cilantro
½ cup freshly squeezed lemon juice
½ cup salsa (choose your degree of heat)
Freshly ground black pepper to taste

This is great served with the Swiss Corn Muffins. Page 74)

1. In a heavy skillet, melt the butter over moderate heat. Cook the shrimp for 2-3 minutes, turning them frequently, until they are firm and pink. Transfer the shrimp to a bowl and set aside.
2. Add all other ingredients to skillet. Cook over low heat for 5 minutes, or until onions are soft and transparent.
3. Return shrimp to skillet. Cook, stirring, until shrimp are heated through.
4. Serve over spinach, pasta or rice.

Smoked Trout Hash

with Poached Eggs

8 servings

1 pound smoked trout, flaked
½ cup sweet onion, chopped
½ cup cooked wild rice
1 cup chopped fresh spinach
1 teaspoon chili powder
½ teaspoon white pepper
Salt to taste
1 cup uncooked fresh hash browns
2 eggs—lightly beaten
2 tablespoons vegetable oil
8 eggs
2 cups Hollandaise sauce (see recipe on page 106)

Garnish—

Dried parsley
8 lemon wedges

Note: We often poach eggs in a fresh vegetable or chicken stock instead of plain water. It gives them a wonderful flavor.

1. Combine first 9 ingredients. Form into 8 patties.
2. Grill on each side, on hot griddle or heavy sauté pan in vegetable oil until hash browns are golden brown.
3. As patties are grilling, poach the eggs.
4. Remove patties from grill. Place a poached egg on top of each patty. Ladle ¼ cup hollandaise over each egg.
5. Sprinkle parsley on top, and serve with a wedge of lemon.

Fish Stock

2 quarts

⅔ cup minced carrots
⅔ cup minced celery
⅔ cup minced onion
2 tablespoons butter
  salt and pepper to taste
2 pounds fish bones and heads
1 bottle dry white wine
2 bay leaves
4 sprigs parsley
1 tablespoon minced fresh dill
  weed
1 tablespoon minced fresh
  thyme
Water to cover

1. Sauté the carrots, celery and onion in the 2 tablespoons butter until onion is opaque. Season to taste with salt and pepper.
2. Transfer to a large saucepan or stock pot, add fish bones, heads and wine. Bring to a boil and skim.
3. Add bay leaves, parsley, dill weed, thyme and enough water to cover. Simmer for 2 hours.
4. Strain through a cloth and use this liquid stock for sauces, soups, etc.

Old Rittenhouse Inn

Side Dishes

Stuffed Pumpkin

8 servings

1 pumpkin, the diameter of a 9-
   inch glass pie plate
1 medium chopped onion
1 cup chopped celery
1 cup slivered mushrooms
4 tablespoons butter
¼ cup sunflower seeds
½ cup cashews
Thyme, sage, rosemary, parsley,
   to taste
½ cup grated cheddar cheese
½ cup grated swiss cheese
2 cups wild rice, cooked in
   chicken stock
1 pint half and half cream

1. Select a cooking pumpkin which will fit on a 9 inch glass pie plate. Make sure it has a flat bottom, so it will sit straight on the pan.
2. Cut the lid, making sure the edges are angled toward the center. Remove seeds and scrape clean.
3. In a large skillet, sauté onions and celery in the butter until they are tender. Add sunflower seeds, cashews, and seasonings. Stir well.
4. In a small skillet, sauté the mushrooms.
5. Layer ingredients into the pumpkin, beginning with wild rice, then mushrooms, then vegetables, then cheeses. Repeat until full. Press all ingredients firmly into the pumpkin, so there is no empty space. Pour half and half over filling. Fit pumpkin lid on top.
6. Bake at 350 degrees for 1 hour or until pumpkin is fork tender.
7 If there is extra stuffing, bake it alongside the pumpkin.

Maple Spiced Squash

8 servings

4 cups butternut or buttercup
   squash
¼ cup soft butter
½ teaspoon nutmeg or to taste
¼ teaspoon allspice or to taste
¼ teaspoon cumin or to taste
1 cup chopped walnuts
1 cup maple syrup
¼ cup melted butter

1. Cut squash in half and remove the seeds.
2. Cover with foil and bake at 350 degrees for one hour or until fork tender.
3. Remove from oven, scoop out pulp and discard the shell.
4. In an electric mixer fitted with a paddle combine squash with butter, nutmeg, and allspice.
5. Whip until smooth at medium speed.
6. On low speed, fold in the walnuts, maple syrup, and melted butter. Mix until smooth.
7. Remove from mixer. Place in oiled baking pan or casserole. Return to oven and heat until hot throughout.

Carrots Lyonnaise

6 servings

**3 cups peeled carrots, cut in
  julienne strips**
4 cups chicken stock
¼ cup butter
1 cup chopped onions
¼ teaspoon salt
¼ teaspoon white pepper
**6 ounces shredded cheddar
  cheese,**
2 lightly beaten eggs
½ cup milk

1. Preheat oven to 350 degrees.
2. Cook carrots in chicken stock for 10 minutes or until tender. Drain.
3. In a medium sized saucepan, melt butter, add onions, and sauté for 5 minutes over medium heat. Season with salt and pepper and reduce heat.
4. Add cheese, eggs, and milk. Cook until cheese is melted, then fold in carrots.
5. Pour into a greased 1½ quart casserole. Bake at 350 degrees for 45 minutes.

Leeks au Gratin

6 servings

4 cups leeks cut into ¼ inch
  pieces
Salt and pepper to taste
½ teaspoon ground thyme
½ teaspoon ground oregano
10 tablespoons butter
4 tablespoons flour
1 cup heavy cream
½ pound bacon, fried until
  crispy (optional)
2 egg yolks
½ cup light cream
¾ cup grated swiss cheese
¾ cup grated cheddar cheese

*At the Rittenhouse we use the first
wild leeks of spring. The rest of
the year, we use the larger
traditional leeks.*

1. Preheat oven to 375 degrees.
2. In a skillet sauté leeks, salt, pepper, thyme, and oregano in 5 tablespoons of butter until leeks are tender.
3. Melt the remaining butter in a saucepan. Stir in flour until smooth. Add the heavy cream, and cook until thickened, stirring constantly with a wire whisk. When mixture comes to a boil, fold in the leeks and bacon. Remove from heat.
4. In another saucepan, whip yolks and light cream together. Pour into leek mixture.
5. Turn into a shallow, buttered, ovenproof dish. Sprinkle with cheeses.
6. Bake at 375 degrees for 20 minutes, or until golden brown.

Eggplant Parmesan

6 servings

1 cup spanish onion, thinly
  sliced
1 bulb of fresh garlic, peeled and
  minced
2 tablespoons olive oil
4 cups tomatoes chopped
12 ounces tomato paste
1 tablespoon fresh basil
1 tablespoon fresh rosemary
1 teaspoon fresh sage
1 teaspoon oregano
Salt and ground fresh pepper to
  taste
Pinch of ground mace
1 or 2 medium-sized eggplants,
  peeled
Flour to coat eggplant
Olive or vegetable oil to brown
  eggplant
2 cups grated parmesan cheese
2 cups grated mozzarella cheese
2 cups bread crumbs

1. Sauté onion and half the garlic in olive oil until onions are opaque.
2. Add remaining garlic, tomatoes and tomato paste. Simmer 3 minutes.
3. Add seasonings and simmer 30 more minutes. Check seasonings and adjust to taste.
4. While sauce is cooking, slice eggplant in pieces about ¼ inch thick. Dry thoroughly with paper towels. Let sit 30 minutes, covered, and dry again.
5. Preheat oven to 350 degrees.
6. Dredge eggplant in flour and brown in oil on both sides until crisp. Drain well.
7. Oil a 2½ quart baking dish. Alternate layers of sauce, eggplant slices, parmesan, sauce, bread crumbs and mozzarella. Continue this order, finishing with sauce and cheeses.
8. Bake for 30 minutes and serve.

Potato Röesti

12-16 patties

1 pound raw hashbrowns
1 cup bread crumbs
½ pound grated onions
3 eggs, lightly beaten
¼ cup chives, chopped fine
1 teaspoon fresh dill weed
   chopped fine
Salt and pepper to taste
Oil for grilling
1 cup grated swiss cheese

1. Mix hashbrowns, bread crumbs, onions, eggs, chives, dillweed, salt and pepper. Form into patties.
2. Heat oil on grill or in a skillet. Grill the patties 4 minutes on one side. Turn over and grill 2 minutes. Then sprinkle with cheese and grill until melted.
3. Remove from skillet and serve at once.

148

Baked Wild Rice

8 servings

2 cups wild rice
½ cup red bell pepper
1 cup chopped fresh spinach
1 cup chopped fresh
   mushrooms
¼ cup chopped fresh parsley
¼ cup minced onion
¼ cup butter
1 cup heavy cream
1 cup grated ricotta cheese
¼ cup toasted almonds
½ cup water chestnuts
3 whole eggs, lightly beaten
1 teaspoon salt
½ teaspoon ground pepper
1 teaspoon ground savory
¼ teaspoon fresh grated
   nutmeg
½ cup fine bread crumbs

1. Preheat oven to 325 degrees.
2. Steam wild rice until done.
3. Sauté pepper, spinach, mushrooms, parsley and onions in butter. Stir in remaining ingredients except bread crumbs.
4. Mix in prepared rice.
5. Turn into a buttered 2½ quart baking dish, cover with foil and bake at 325 degrees for 1 to 1½ hours. Sprinkle with bread crumbs and bake 5 minutes uncovered.

Apple Rice

6 servings

1 cup brown rice, cooked, chilled

1 cup wild rice, cooked in apple cider, chilled

½ cup chopped sweet onion

½ cup chopped celery

1 cup slivered apples, cored, unpeeled

2 tablespoons brown sugar

½ cup chopped dates

½ cup golden raisins soaked 2 hours in dry sherry

¼ cup chopped broccoli

⅓ cup chopped almonds

⅓ cup roquefort cheese

¼ teaspoon ground cardamom

¼ teaspoon ground turmeric

⅛ teaspoon ground cumin

Great accompaniment with pork or game.

This is great served as a side dish; but it is equally nice as a salad with the chutney dressing. Or add 2 cups coarsely chopped cooked boned breast of chicken for a lunch salad.

1. Combine all ingredients and toss until well blended.

Bayfield Apple Sauce

makes 2 quarts

5 pounds apples (Wealthy or Mackintosh)
1 cup apple juice
¹/₃ cup lemon juice
¼ teaspoon ground nutmeg
¼ teaspoon ground cinnamon
¼ teaspoon ground allspice
1½ cups crab apple jelly (see recipe on page 84)

1. Pare, core and quarter the apples.
2. Mix with apple juice, lemon juice, and spices in a large saucepan. Cook over medium heat until very soft.
3. Remove from heat. Process in a food processor, using a steel blade, until smooth. Add jelly. Process until color is evenly distributed (3-5 seconds).

Black Beans and Rice

8 servings

1 pound dried black beans
Water to cover
2 tablespoons butter
4 cloves garlic, peeled and
    minced
1 teaspoon cumin
2 cups beef stock
1 cup chopped onion
1 tablespoon butter
1 tablespoon vinegar
1 teaspoon salt
$^1\!/_3$ cup salsa, hot or medium
$^1\!/_8$ teaspoon hot pepper sauce
3 cups cooked yellow rice

1. Wash beans, drain, and place in large sauce-pan. Cover with water and soak overnight. Drain beans.
2. Melt butter in a large saucepan. Add beans, garlic, cumin, beef stock, and simmer over low heat until beans are tender (about 1 hour). Remove from heat, drain well and return to saucepan.
3. In small skillet, sauté the onion in 1 table-spoon butter until opaque.
4. Add onions to beans. Then add vinegar, salt to taste, salsa and hot pepper sauce.
5. Serve over rice accompanied by extra salsa.

Fettucini Florentine

serves 8

3 eggs, lightly beaten
1½ cup sour cream
½ cup heavy whipping cream
3 cups cooked fettucini, al dente or firm to the bite
4 cups fresh chopped spinach
2 cups shredded monterey jack cheese
1-2 cups grated parmesan cheese

1. Preheat oven to 350 degrees.
2. Process eggs, sour cream, heavy cream in food processor fitted with a steel blade.
3. Lightly toss fettucini and spinach in a large bowl.
4. Add cream mixture to pasta and spinach. Stir in monterey jack cheese.
5. Put in buttered baking dish and sprinkle parmesan cheese on top. Bake in 350 degree oven for 15-20 minutes.

Tomato-Zucchini Pasta

8 servings

3 cups cooked pasta
1½ cups chopped, unpeeled
   tomatoes
1½ cups chopped, peeled
   zucchini
4 cloves garlic, minced
¼ cup chopped green onions
½ cup hot salsa
1-1½ cups Basil-Tomato Sauce
   (see recipe on page 103)
1 tablespoon lemon juice
2 cups grated mozzarella cheese

1. Preheat oven to 300 degrees.
2. Combine tomatoes, zucchini, garlic, onions, salsa, basil-tomato sauce and lemon.
3. In a 1½ quart buttered baking dish, alternate layers of pasta and tomato mixture. Finish with mixture. Sprinkle cheese on top.
4. Bake at 300 degrees for 15 minutes, or until cheese is melted and pasta is hot throughout.

Old Rittenhouse Inn

Desserts

Lemon Cheesecake

with Glazed Raspberries

1 cheesecake

Shell—

2 cups flour
½ cup sugar
2 teaspoons grated lemon rind
½ pound softened butter
2 large egg yolks
½ teaspoon vanilla

Filling—

2½ pounds softened
   cream cheese
1¾ cups sugar
1 teaspoon grated lemon rind
¼ teaspoon vanilla
2 tablespoons flour
½ teaspoon salt
4 large eggs
2 large egg yolks
½ cup heavy cream

Topping—

¾ cup of water
¾ cup sugar
3 tablespoons cornstarch
2 tablespoons light corn syrup
3-4 drops of red food coloring
4 cups red raspberries

Garnish—

sour cream
red raspberries
confectioner's sugar

Pictured on page 9 of
Old Rittenhouse History.

SHELL
1. In a bowl, combine flour, sugar, lemon rind, and butter.
2. Add egg yolks, vanilla. Form a dough.
3. Remove ring from 10-inch spring form pan.
4. Press ⅓ dough on to the bottom of the springform pan, bake in a preheated 400-degree oven for 8 minutes.
5. Let it cool on a rack.
6. Return ring to pan, and pat the remaining dough into the sides of the pan.

FILLING
1. Preheat oven to 425 degrees.
2. Beat the softened cream cheese, sugar, lemon rind, and vanilla until smooth.
3. Beat in flour, salt. Add eggs, and egg yolks, one at a time. Stir in the cream.
4. Pour the filling into the shell and place a pan of water under the cheesecake. Bake in a 425-degree oven for 15 minutes. Reduce heat to 300 degrees and bake for 1½ hours more.
5. Remove from oven. Cool to room temperature. Then place in refrigerator to chill.

TOPPING
1. Combine ¾ cup water, sugar, and cornstarch. Cook over moderately high heat until thick and clear.
2. Remove from heat. Stir in the corn syrup and food coloring. Let topping cool until lukewarm.
3. Arrange raspberries on top of cheesecake. Pour the topping over them.
4. Chill overnight.
5. Serve with garnish of sour cream, red raspberries, and a dusting of confectioner's sugar.

Wisconsin Cheese Pie

one 9-inch pie

Pie—

1 unbaked nine-inch pie shell
12 ounces cottage cheese
   or ricotta
16 ounces softened
   cream cheese
1½ cups sugar
1 teaspoon vanilla
1 lemon, seeds removed,
   quartered
4 eggs, slightly beaten

Garnish—

Whipped cream
Fresh strawberries

Note: At the Rittenhouse we serve Wisconsin Cheese Pie topped with apple cider marmalade (see page 81), slivered apples, and whipped cream. This is one of our most requested pies on our menu.

1. Preheat oven to 350 degrees.
2. Combine all ingredients except eggs. Blend in food processor until smooth.
3. Fold in eggs.
4. Pour into pie shell. Bake at 350 degrees for 30 minutes.
5. Cool completely before serving.
6. Garnish.

Maple Walnut Pie

one 9-inch pie

1 nine-inch pie shell
4 tablespoons melted butter
½ cup sugar
1 cup maple syrup
4 eggs, beaten
1 teaspoon vanilla extract
⅛ teaspoon coffee extract
  (optional)
1⅓ cups chopped walnuts

Note: For best results, use a glass pie dish.

1. Preheat oven to 350 degrees.
2. Mix all ingredients, and pour into the pie shells.
3. Bake at 350 degrees for 20 minutes. Reduce heat to 300 degrees and bake until the center of the filling is set, and the crust is golden brown.
4. Cool well. Serve with whipped cream and a drizzle of maple syrup or with a scoop of maple walnut ice cream.

Pictured on page 14 of Old Rittenhouse History.

Lemon Chess Pie

two 9-inch pies

**2 prepared, unbaked nine-inch
   pie shells
6 cups sugar
6 tablespoons flour
6 tablespoons cornmeal
12 eggs, lightly beaten
¾ cup melted butter
¾ cup heavy cream
3-4 whole lemons**

1. Preheat oven 350 degrees.
2. Mix together sugar, flour, and cornmeal in a medium size mixing bowl.
3. Grate peeling of lemons and set aside. Cut peeled lemons in half and remove seeds. Squeeze the juice from each lemon half into a small bowl and set aside. Save remaining pulp.
4. Mix eggs, butter, cream, grated lemon peel, and squeezed lemon juice in a large mixing bowl.
5. In a food processor, fitted with a steel blade, process the rest of the lemon pulp until fine. Fold into the wet ingredients.
6. Add dry ingredients to wet. Stir until mixed.
7. Turn into pie shells and bake in preheated 350-degree oven 35-45 minutes. Remove from oven and cool to room temperature. Then refrigerate to set the pie.

Pumpkin Walnut Pie

one 9-inch pie

Pie—

1 unbaked 9-inch pie shell
2 cups canned or fresh
    pumpkin purée
¾ cup maple syrup
1 tablespoon molasses
½ teaspoon salt
1½ teaspoon cinnamon
1 teaspoon ginger
1 teaspoon allspice
1⅔ cups heavy whipping cream
½ cup chopped walnuts
3 eggs, slightly beaten

Garnish—

Whipped cream
Ground walnuts
Sprinkle of cinnamon sugar

1. Preheat oven to 350 degrees.
2. Blend together the pumpkin, syrup, molasses, salt, cinnamon, ginger, allspice, cream, and walnuts.
3. Fold in eggs.
4. Turn into pie shell.
5. Bake at 350 degrees until knife inserted into center of the pie comes out clean.
6. Cool completely before serving.
7. Garnish.

Apple Butter Pie

one 9-inch pie

Pie—

1 nine-inch unbaked pie shell
1 tablespoon molasses
¼ cup honey
¾ cup maple syrup
¼ cup apple juice
1 tablespoon lemon juice
8-9 cups of peeled and
   sliced apples
¼ cup melted butter
¼ cup flour

Streusel Topping—

1 cup raw oatmeal
¼ cup brown sugar
¼ cup flour
¼ cup softened butter
¼ cup chopped English Walnuts
½ teaspoon ground cinnamon
½ teaspoon ground nutmeg
½ teaspoon ground ginger
½ teaspoon vanilla extract

PIE

1. Preheat oven to 300 degrees.
2. Combine molasses, honey, maple syrup, apple juice, and lemon. Bring to a boil. Reduce heat to a medium heat.
3. Add apples. Cook until tender, stirring occasionally. Drain apples, reserving syrup.
4. Stir flour into butter until smooth. Blend butter and flour into syrup. Return to low heat and cook until thick and smooth.
5. Fold apples into thickened syrup. Cool to lukewarm temperature.
6. Fold into 9-inch unbaked pie shell.
7. Sprinkle streusel topping on top of filling and bake at 300 degrees for 10 to 15 minutes until the crust and topping is a golden brown.

TOPPING

1. In your mixer, fitted with a paddle, blend until well combined.

Cranberry Surprise Pie

two 9-inch pies

2 nine-inch unbaked pie shells
½ cup sour cream
½ cup softened cream cheese
½ cup corn starch
¼ cup fresh lime juice
¼ cup fresh orange juice
¼ cup lemonade concentrate
¼ cup cranberry concentrate
1½ cups honey
2 cups fresh or frozen
   cranberries
1 tablespoon grated lemon peel
1 tablespoon grated orange peel
4 cups diced apples
   (peeled, quartered and cored)

1. Preheat oven to 350 degrees.
2. Combine first 8 ingredients in processor, using a steel blade. Blend until smooth.
3. Add cranberries. Pulse until chopped.
4. Add lemon and orange peels. Blend 2 seconds.
5. Remove from processor.
6. Put apples in a large mixing bowl. Stir in the above mixture.
7. Pour into two 9-inch pie shells. Bake at 350 degrees for 15-20 minutes or until filling begins to set.
8. Remove from oven and add streusel topping (see recipe on page 164). Return to oven. Reduce heat to 300 degrees and bake until center feels firm to the touch; 30-45 minutes.
9. Remove from oven. Serve warm with vanilla ice cream.

Black Walnut Bourbon Pie

one 9-inch pie

1 nine-inch unbaked pie shell
3 eggs
1¼ cups sugar
1 cup dark corn syrup
¼ cup bourbon
½ cup melted butter
¾ cup chopped English walnuts
½ cup black walnut pieces
6 ounces semi-sweet chocolate,
  melted

1. Preheat oven to 375 degrees.
2. Beat eggs, sugar and corn syrup.
3. Add bourbon, butter, all walnuts, and chocolate.
4. Pour into pie shell. Bake in a 375-degree oven for 15 minutes. Reduce heat to 325 degrees and bake until filling is lightly set, and crust is golden (35 to 45 minutes).
5. Remove from oven. Cool to room temperature. Then refrigerate to complete setting.
6. Serve warm with vanilla ice cream. This pie is extremely rich, and will easily serve 10.

Streusel Topping

3 cups

2 cups rolled oats
½ cup brown sugar (light or dark)
½ cup flour
½ cup softened butter
½ cup finely chopped walnuts
1 teaspoon ground cinnamon
1 teaspoon ground nutmeg
1 teaspoon ground ginger
1 teaspoon vanilla extract

This makes enough streusel topping to cover two 9-inch pies.

1. Combine oats, sugar, flour, and butter in an electric mixer. Blend with paddle attachment until ingredients are evenly mixed.
2. Add walnuts, spices, and vanilla and mix well.

Orange Blossom Torte

1 torte

Torte—

9 eggs, separated
1 cup sugar
1 tablespoon lemon juice
1 ½ cups all-purpose flour
1 ounce white chocolate, melted
½ cup butter, melted and
  slightly cooled
Orange liqueur

Filling—

½ cup dairy sour cream
1 eight-ounce package cream
  cheese, softened
1 cup butter, softened
¼ teaspoon grated orange peel
½ teaspoon orange extract
1 cup powdered sugar

Frosting—

1 ½ cups whipping cream
1 teaspoon vanilla
¼ teaspoon walnut extract
Orange food coloring

Garnish—

orange slices
fresh flowers

*One of the Old Rittenhouse Inn's
most requested desserts.*

*Pictured on page 14 of
Old Rittenhouse History.*

TORTE

1. In large mixer bowl, beat egg whites to soft peaks. Gradually add sugar, beating until stiff peaks form. Set aside. Wash beaters.
2. In small mixer bowl fitted with beaters, beat yolks at high speed for 6 minutes or till thick and lemon colored. Add lemon juice. Carefully fold yolk mixture into egg whites. Gradually fold flour into egg mixture. Fold in chocolate and butter.
3. Turn mixture into two 8-inch round baking pans. Bake in a 325-degree oven for 30 minutes or till cake tests done. Invert cake in pan; cool thoroughly.
4. Loosen cake; remove from pans. Split each layer in half horizontally, and brush with orange liqueur.

FILLING

1. In a medium mixer bowl fitted with paddle, combine dairy sour cream, cream cheese, and butter. Beat until fluffy.
2. Beat in grated orange peel, orange extract, and powdered sugar.
3. Place one split cake layer on plate. Spread about ¾ cup filling on top. Continue with remaining layers, placing each on the preceeding layer and cover with filling.

FROSTING

1. Combine whipping cream, vanilla, walnut extract, and a few drops orange food coloring.
2. Whip to stiff peaks.
3. Frost completed cake. If desired, garnish with orange slices and flowers.

Jam Cakes

24 cakes

Cake—

1 cup shortening
1 teaspoon almond extract
1 teaspoon vanilla extract
1 cup white corn syrup
3 cups white flour
2 teaspoons baking powder
1 teaspoon cinnamon
1 teaspoon allspice
2 eggs, lightly beaten
½ cup chopped toasted almonds
1 cup strawberry or red raspberry jam

Frosting—

10 ounces cream cheese softened
¼ cup (4 tablespoons) unsalted butter, softened
1 cup confectioner's sugar
⅓ cup whipping cream at room temperature

CAKE

1. Preheat oven to 350 degrees.
2. Grease a 7x12 inch cake pan.
3. In electric mixer fitted with paddle, combine shortening and extracts. Add corn syrup. Mix well.
4. In another bowl mix by hand the flour, baking powder, and spices. Add to the first mixture. Add egg and mix well.
5. Spread one half of the dough into a greased pan. Spread jam evenly over dough and sprinkle with almonds. Cover with remaining dough.
6. Bake in 350-degree oven for about 30 minutes. Frost and cut in squares.

FROSTING

1. Cream the cream cheese and butter in small mixing bowl of an electric mixer, fitted with a paddle, until fluffy and light. Scrape bottom and sides of bowl with rubber spatula at least once.
2. With mixer on low speed, add confectioner's sugar until incorporated. Scrape bowl and whip 30 seconds at high speed.
3. Return mixer to low speed and add the cream slowly. Mix until incorporated.
4. Increase the speed and beat the frosting until fluffy.

Pot de Crème au Chocolate

8 cups

8 ounces softened cream cheese
¼ pound (1 stick) unsalted butter, softened
½ cup sour cream
1 cup powdered cocoa
½ cup powdered sugar
¼ cup Kahlua
¼ cup Amaretto
¼ cup Grand Marnier
2 teaspoons vanilla
2 drops of almond extract
2 drops of orange extract
4 cups whipped cream (sweetened and stiffly whipped)

Garnish—

Whipped cream, sweetened
Almonds
Shaved chocolate

1. Cream the cheese, butter and sour cream in a mixer, using paddle on low speed. Scrape down sides of mixing bowl, and beat until the mixture is creamy.
2. Slowly add the cocoa, sugar, Kahlua, Amaretto, Grand Marnier, vanilla, and the extracts, continuing to mix at low speed.
3. Remove mixture from bowl and chill.
4. Just before serving, fold an equal amount of whipped cream into the batter. If you prefer a more chocolatey, bittersweet pot du crème, use less whipped cream.
5. Serve topped with whipped cream, slivered almonds, and shaved chocolate.
6. This recipe makes 16 servings. For eight servings, simply reserve one-half of the chocolate mixture for another time. The chocolate mixture can be stored in a refrigerator for 7-10 days, as long as the whipped cream has not been added.

Bayfield Strawberry Mousse

8 servings

½ cup egg whites
½ cup sugar
2½ cups sliced and hulled
strawberries
1½ cups heavy sweetened
cream, whipped
3 ounces tangerine or orange
liqueur (optional)

Garnish—

Fresh strawberries
Powdered sugar

This also makes a great pie filling. Simply fill a graham or chocolate crumb crust and garnish with more berries.

1. Whip egg whites and sugar until stiff.
2. Fold strawberries into whites and sugar.
3. Fold whipped cream and liqueur into mixture.
4. Chill or freeze if you prefer.
5. Serve in chilled glasses.
6. Garnish with strawberries.

Winter Snow-Eggs

in Red Raspberry Sauce

6 servings

Eggs—

1 tablespoon unflavored gelatin
¼ cup cold water
1 cup boiling water
¾ cup fine white sugar
¼ cup strained lemon juice
1 tablespoon grated lemon rind
3 large egg whites
½ pint heavy whipping cream
1 tablespoon walnut or hazelnut oil

Sauce—

16 ounces red raspberry jelly
½ cup honey

Garnish—

Whole fresh red raspberries
Mint leaves

EGGS

1. Sprinkle gelatin over cold water in a two cup measure, stir and let soften 5 minutes.
2. Add gelatin to boiling water. Dissolve and then add sugar, lemon juice, and rind. Blend well.
3. Chill in refrigerator, stirring occasionally, until mixture thickens (about 2 hours; although this can be sped up by placing on ice or in freezer).
4. As gelatin mixture is very thick and syrupy, beat egg whites in medium sized bowl fitted with beaters until stiff and shiny.
5. Add gelatin mixture slowly to egg whites, beating continually. Turn up to medium high speed and whip until very stiff peaks form. This takes awhile, so be patient.
6. In a separate bowl, beat cream until stiff. Gently fold cream into gelatin mixture.
7. Brush muffin tins with flavored oil and fill with mixture. Chill several hours.

SAUCE

1. Combine jelly and honey. Heat until softened. Cool to room temperature.
2. Remove snow-eggs from muffin pans by running a thin bladed spatula around edge. Place on chilled glass plates. Form into slightly elongated "egg" shape with a lightly oiled spoon. Ladle raspberry sauce over each egg and garnish with red raspberries and fresh mint; or make a pool of sauce on the plate, center the egg on the sauce and top with raspberries and fresh mint.

Baked Apples

6 servings

Baked Apples—

6 large baking apples
⅓ cup brown sugar
1 teaspoon cinnamon
1 teaspoon nutmeg
1 teaspoon allspice
1 cup cranberry chutney (see recipe on page 92)

Applejack Cream—

1½ cups heavy whipping cream
½ cup Applejack liqueur, or any apple flavored liqueur
¼ teaspoon cinnamon
¼ teaspoon nutmeg

BAKED APPLES
1. Preheat oven to 325 degrees.
2. Stem and core apples ⅔ of the way through from top.
3. Combine sugar and spices.
4. Stuff apples ⅔ full with chutney. Fill with sugar and spice mixture.
5. Place on rack in baking pan. Pour water in pan ½-inch in depth. Bake at 325 degrees for 45 minutes or until apples are tender. Remove from oven.
6. Serve on a bed of Applejack cream.

APPLEJACK CREAM
Blend all ingredients until smooth. Serve warm.

Maple Glazed Pears

6-8 servings

Pears—

6-8 pears, peeled, cored and halved
Rind from 1 orange, cut into julienne strips, (all white removed)
2 cups maple syrup
½ cup orange juice concentrate
¼ cup orange liqueur

Garnish—

1 cup sweetened whipped cream
½ cup chopped walnuts

About the end of August, Bayfield's pears ripen to a golden yellow. The combination of orange liqueur and maple syrup is delicious.

PEARS
1. Combine rind, syrup, juice concentrate, and liqueur in a saucepan. Bring to a boil, and cook for ten minutes to thicken.
2. Reduce heat, add pears and simmer for ten minutes or until pears are tender.
3. Remove from heat. Cool slightly.
4. Serve on a dollop of freshly whipped cream, topped with a sprinkle of chopped walnuts and drizzled with the pear sauce.

Wild Rice Custard Pudding

8 servings

Custard—

4 eggs
1 cup brown sugar
1 teaspoon vanilla extract
1 teaspoon almond extract
1 tablespoon Irish Mist liqueur
1 quart milk
2 cups cooked wild rice

Garnish—

1 cup whipped cream,
   sweetened with maple syrup.
Chopped walnuts

1. Preheat oven to 325 degrees.
2. Blend eggs, sugar, extracts and liqueurs.
3. Add milk and stir in wild rice. Pour into custard molds. Place molds in a sheet cake pan in the center of the oven and fill with warm water to ½ inch. Bake at 325 degrees until set (about 1 hour, 15 minutes).
4. Serve topped with sweetened whipped cream and chopped walnuts.

Cranberry Sherbet

1½ quarts

12 ounces frozen or fresh cranberries
1 cup orange juice concentrate
1-1½ cups sugar (to taste)
½ cup lemonade concentrate
2 cups heavy whipping cream
2 tablespoons freshly grated lemon peel
30 ounces (3 ten-ounce bottles) mineral water

Notes: The sherbet will be creamier if the freezing process takes place slowly. (45 minutes.)

We have also done this recipe with dried cranberries with good results. Simply substitute the frozen cranberries with 6-8 ounces of dried cranberries.

1. Bring cranberries and orange juice concentrate to a boil in saucepan. Cook on medium heat for 1 minute or until the berries pop. Remove from heat. Cool to room temperature and refrigerate.
2. When chilled, transfer mixture to food processor fitted with steel blade. Add the remaining ingredients and blend until smooth.
3. Remove from processor. Transfer mixture into a 2-quart ice cream freezer.
4. Freeze according to manufacturer's directions.

Cranberry Cookies

5 dozen cookies

1 cup butter, softened, at room
   temperature
1 cup brown sugar
1 cup white sugar
3 eggs, lightly beaten
1 teaspoon vanilla
2 teaspoons baking soda in ¼
   cup hot water
2⅔ cups rolled oats
3 cups flour
1 cup chopped English walnuts
2 cups chopped fresh or frozen
   cranberries
½ cup grated orange peel
¼ cup grated lemon peel

1. Preheat oven to 350 degrees and lightly grease cookie sheets.
2. Cream butter and sugars.
3. Add eggs, vanilla, and baking soda.
4. Add oats and flour. Mix well.
5. Add walnuts, cranberries and peel. Chill dough for 45 minutes.
6. Roll dough into balls and place on cookie sheet.
7. Bake for 10-15 minutes.

Wild Rice Cookies

6 dozen small or 2 dozen large cookies

1 egg
1½ cups softened butter
2 cups brown sugar
¼ cup lemon juice
1 tablespoon vanilla
¼ teaspoon almond extract
2 tablespoons bourbon
   (optional)
4 cups all-purpose flour
½ teaspoon salt
1 teaspoon soda
1 cup well cooked wild rice, well
   drained

These cookies are excellent with a glaze made of lemon juice and powdered sugar.

1. Preheat oven to 350 degrees.
2. Cream together egg, butter, sugar, lemon juice, vanilla, almond extract, and bourbon.
3. In a separate mixing bowl combine flour, salt, baking soda, and cooked wild rice.
4. Mix dry ingredients with wet. Form into cookies. Bake on greased cookie sheet 10 to 15 minutes.

Molasses Cookies

100 three-inch cookies

1½ cups softened butter
1½ cups granulated sugar
1½ cups dark molasses
1 teaspoon ground cinnamon
1 tablespoon ground ginger
½ tablespoon salt
1 tablespoon baking soda
6 cups flour

1. Preheat oven to 350 degrees and grease cookie sheets.
2. Cream the butter and sugar. Add molasses and mix.
3. In a separate bowl, combine spices, salt, baking soda, and flour.
4. Add the dry ingredients to the sugar mixture and blend well.
5. Roll out dough on a pastry cloth, using granulated white sugar to prevent sticking and give a sugary look to the cookies.
6. Bake on a lightly greased cookie sheet at 350 degrees for 8-12 minutes. Loosen from pan with a spatula while still warm. Cool on a wire rack. Store in an airtight container.

Red Raspberry Truffles

36 truffles

½ cup sweetened condensed milk
½ cup light cream
5 ounces high quality* semi-sweet chocolate, melted
4 ounces unsweetened chocolate, melted
2 egg yolks
2 tablespoons almond liqueur
2 tablespoons red raspberry liqueur (may be purchased at a liquor store, or the recipe on page 180 may be used)
36 fresh red raspberries

Roll Truffles in:

Cocoa powder
Powdered sugar
Chopped nuts

Note: The quality of the chocolate is of utmost importance—Don't skimp.

1. Combine sweetened condensed milk and cream in a heavy, medium-sized saucepan. Bring just to boiling. Remove from heat and cool 5 minutes.
2. Combine milk mixture with both chocolates in a food processor bowl with a steel blade. Process 5-10 seconds. Scrape down.
3. Add egg yolks and process 5 seconds. Scrape down.
4. Add liqueurs and process 5 seconds.
5. Pour mixture into a small mixing bowl. Place bowl in a larger container with ice packed around the smaller bowl. Be sure no ice or water gets into the mixture!
6. Stir until thick and completely cooled.
7. Remove smaller bowl from ice and whip with electric mixer, fitted with a paddle, about 2 minutes, or until stiff peaks form. Chill until firm (about 1 hour).
8. Use 1 tablespoon of mixture for each truffle. Shape into a ball around a fresh red raspberry. Roll in cocoa powder, chopped nuts, or powdered sugar.
9. Store in a dry cool place.

Pictured on page 14 of Old Rittenhouse History.

Old Rittenhouse Inn

Beverages

Red Raspberry Cordial

8 cups

4 cups fresh red raspberries
4 cups sugar
2 cups gin or vodka

1. Combine ingredients and stir well in a one gallon jar.
2. Cover tightly and store in a cool, dark place. Stir once a week for 4 months.
3. Strain through a cheesecloth and bottle for use.

Red Raspberry Cream

4-6 servings

4 ounces red raspberry cordial
(see recipe on page 180)
6 ounces chilled heavy cream
8 ounces chilled club soda

Garnish—

1 pint fresh red raspberries

1. Blend cordial, cream, and soda in a blender, or food processor until it is foamy.
2. Pour in a chilled, stemmed glass.
3. Garnish with red raspberries.

Mulled Apple Cider
1 quart

1 quart fresh cider
½ pint cranberry juice
¼ cup sugar
½ teaspoon ground cinnamon
¼ teaspoon ground allspice
¼ teaspoon ground ginger
¼ teaspoon ground nutmeg
¼ teaspoon ground white
　pepper
Pinch of ground cloves

Garnish—

Cinnamon sticks

1. Heat cider in a large kettle. Add cranberry juice, sugar, and spices.
2. Bring to a boil. Reduce heat and simmer 30 minutes. Remove from heat. Skim off spices which have risen to the top or strain through cheesecloth.
3. Serve hot, garnished with a cinnamon stick.

Strawberry Mimosa

six 8-ounce servings

12 ounces frozen strawberries,
   partially thawed
6 ounces orange juice
12 ounces sparkling white grape
   juice
24 ounces champagne

Garnish—

6 whole fresh strawberries
6 mint leaves

1. Combine berries and juice in a blender or food processor fitted with a steel blade. Blend until smooth.
2. Fill 6 stemmed 8-ounce glasses half full with the berry mixture.
3. Fill each glass with champagne.
4. Garnish each glass with a strawberry and a sprig of fresh mint.

Hot Chocolate

6 servings

6 cups milk
⅛ teaspoon salt
¾ cup powdered cocoa
⅔ cup sugar
1 tablespoon vanilla extract
⅛ teaspoon ground cinnamon

Garnish—

Whipped cream
Shaved chocolate

Optional—

⅔ cup Amaretto or ⅔ cup orange liqueur

1. Combine milk, salt, cocoa, sugar. Heat until just below boiling temperature, stirring constantly. Remove from heat.
2. Stir in vanilla and cinnamon. As an option, one of the two liqueurs may be added.
3. Ladle into cups. Garnish with whipped cream and shaved chocolate.

Chocolate Mint Tea

makes 4 cups

2 cups brewed mint tea
2 cups hot chocolate made with milk
½ teaspoon crème de menthe liqueur

Garnish—

Whipped cream
Fresh mint sprigs

1. Blend mint tea and hot chocolate in a saucepan. Heat through.
2. Remove from heat. Add crème de menthe.
3. Serve with a dollop of whipped cream and a sprig of fresh mint.

Chocolate Truffle Cream

4 servings

2 cups chocolate ice cream
3 ounces Chocolate Truffle
  liqueur
1½ ounces Cognac
1 ounce Frangelico

Garnish—

Shaved chocolate

*Vanilla ice cream and White
Chocolate Truffle liqueur may
be substituted.*

1. Combine all ingredients in a blender or food processor fitted with a steel bade. Blend until smooth and creamy.
2. Serve in chilled glasses and garnish with shaved chocolate.

Irish Cream

6-8 servings

1 can sweetened condensed
  milk (8 ounces)
12 ounces heavy whipping
  cream
1 teaspoon almond extract
1½ tablespoons chocolate
  syrup
1 cup Irish Whiskey (8 ounces)

1. Combine all ingredients in food processor fitted with a steel blade, or in blender. Mix until smooth.
2. Pour into chilled stemmed glasses and serve.

Index